Cooking Seafood and Carolina Critters

A Collection of Recipes by
Jerry G. Smith

Chef Dirt
Outer Banks, NC

Printed in 2000

Cover and Recipes
Copyright © 1999
by Jerry G. Smith

Dividers and Cooking Hints
Copyright © 1999
Cookbooks by Morris Press
ISBN #0-9662656-2-9

Printed in the U.S.A. by

P.O. Box 2110 • Kearney, NE 68848

Appreciation

First I would like to thank all my friends that made *Seafood and Things* a success, I am truly honored that you choose to put it in your home.

I am proud to introduce to you my latest book, *Cooking Seafood and Carolina Critters with Chef Dirt and Sugar Britches.* This book is a collection of my brand new recipes, along with some very old recipes given to me by a very dear friend, Elizabeth Repp, of Southern Shores, North Carolina. Thank you Mrs. Repp, and to my mother, Virgie Cox of NewPort News, Virginia. Thank you Mom. And last of all "Sweet Britches," thanks Sweet Britches, for whatever you did.

Introduction

Cooking Seafood and Carolina Critters is a collection of my brand new recipes, most requested by my friends over the past year.

Many of my friends that have purchased *Seafood and Things* have called and asked for specific recipes on things such as Cape Hatteras clam chowder, oyster and crab bisques, I even had one lady that wanted to know how to make a true mint julep. I hope that I have fulfilled everyone's wish.

I just had to include what I call my nostalgia recipes, this is a collection of things I grew up with. You will be able to pick most of them out. For instance; you will notice that many of them call for lard instead of shortening, but many of our grandmothers were very inventive in this area, some would kill and bake a duck for a smoother lard (grease) for baking things such as cookies and cakes, others would make shortening, using butter and lard. Some of these recipes were written down by hand to be passed on, they were such treasures that I could not bring myself to reword them from their original content, the paper they were

written on was very old and fragile, and because the ink had faded, very hard to read. I know you will enjoy reading them, but please do try them, they are as good today as they were in yesteryear.

I remember when margarine first came on the market, the time was in the mid 1940s. It was packaged in a clear cellophane bag with a gob of yellow dye that you had to knead into the white stuff. This was supposed to replace butter. I don't know why they bothered, butter in the country was plentiful and cheap, some farmers used it to grease wheel axles.

Now I want to talk about what I call my ha! ha! recipes. These are recipes for wild game, I really don't expect you to do much cooking with them but I have eaten everything mentioned in them and the recipes are authentic, now if someone should ask how to cook an opossum you can tell them how. Opossums, raccoons, squirrels, and rabbits saved many families from starvation during the depression years. Wild animals and domestic food animals have one thing in common, at one time they were all wild. I think at the very least you will find them interesting reading (baked opossum and sweet potatoes is a gourmet delight, really!) I have a new assistant chef working with me (when she ain't out frog gigging or snake hunting in the alligator swamp area), her name is "Sugar Britches," she has come up with some really good stuff, which I have put in this book. But if she brings one of them gators in my kitchen, she will be on the menu.

Sugar Britches likes to cook critters, go frog gigging, and snake hunting. She is a jewel and I don't know how I ever got along without her cooking expertise. Sugar Britches is destined to become a world renowned chef.

I have tried very hard to make these recipes as simple and easy to follow as I know how, but if you should come across something that has you confused, call me, my home phone number is (252) 491-2403. I truly hope you have as much fun reading and using this book, as I have had writing it.

Jerry G. Smith
Chef Dirt

About the Artist

Vickie Wallace resides in Manteo, North Carolina with her husband and two daughters. She has a Bachelor of Fine Arts degree from Stephen F. Austin St. University in East Texas. She has worked as an advertising designer and has done free-lance artwork for the Santa Ana – Lower Rio Grande Valley National Wildlife Refuge Complex, the Frontera Audubon Society, Alligator River and Pea Island National Wildlife Refuge

Vicki Wallace 99

Cape Hatteras Lighthouse
Buxton, NC

Special Thanks

This is for the most important person in my life, my wife Becky. If it were not for her this book would not exist, she does the marketing, television, radio, and newspaper promotions, not to mention the job of designing, compiling and distributing of all books.

Table of Contents

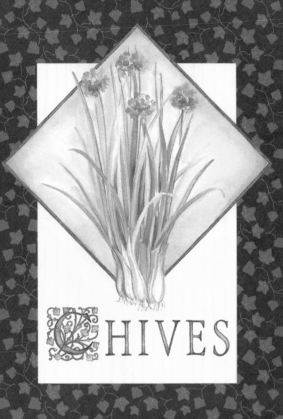

CHIVES

Appetizers
& Beverages

Helpful Hints

- You won't need sugar with your tea if you drink jasmine tea or any of the lighter-bodied varieties, like Formosa Oolong, which have their own natural sweetness. They are fine for sugarless iced tea, too.

- Calorie-free club soda adds sparkle to iced fruit juices, makes them go further and reduces calories per portion.

- For tea flavoring, dissolve old-fashioned lemon drops or hard mint candy in your tea. They melt quickly and keep the tea brisk!

- Most diets call for 8 ounces of milk and 4 ounces of fruit juice. Check your glassware. Having the exact size glass ensures the correct serving amount.

- Make your own spiced tea or cider. Place orange peels, whole cloves, and cinnamon sticks in a 6-inch square piece of cheesecloth. Gather the corners and tie with a string. Steep in hot cider or tea for 10 minutes or longer if you want a stronger flavor.

- Always chill juices or sodas before adding to beverage recipes.

- To cool your punch, float an ice ring made from the punch rather than using ice cubes. Not only is this more decorative, but it also inhibits melting and diluting.

- Place fresh or dried mint in the bottom of a cup of hot chocolate for a cool and refreshing taste.

- One lemon yields about ¼ cup juice; one orange yields about ⅓ cup juice. This is helpful in making fresh orange juice or lemonade!

- Never boil coffee; it brings out the acid and causes a bitter taste. Store ground coffee in the refrigerator or freezer to keep it fresh.

- Always use COLD water for electric drip coffee makers. Use 1 to 2 tablespoons ground coffee for each cup of water.

- Seeds and nuts, both shelled and unshelled, keep best and longest when stored in the freezer. Unshelled nuts crack more easily when frozen. Nuts and seeds can be used directly from the freezer.

- Cheeses should be served at room temperature, approximately 70°.

Appetizers & Beverages

SUGAR COATED PEANUTS

1 c. sugar
½ c. water

3 c. raw peanuts, with skins on
Red food coloring (opt.

Mix all ingredients together in a saucepan and cook over medium heat until all syrup is coated on peanuts, syrup must be all gone. Spread on a baking sheet and place in a 250° oven for 25 minutes. Allow to cool and serve.

CHEF DIRT'S' NUTTY CORN

5 qt. freshly popped popcorn, unsalted
1 c. raw peanuts, skins on
½ c. butter, softened
½ c. margarine, softened
2 c. firmly packed light brown sugar

½ c. dark corn syrup
½ tsp. baking soda
½ tsp. salt
½ tsp. vanilla extract

Mix together the softened butter and margarine and set aside. Meanwhile, combine popcorn and peanuts in a very large baking pan that has been lightly greased with butter, mix well and set aside. Start preheating your oven to 250°. Melt the butter and margarine mixture in a large saucepan; stir in the brown sugar and corn syrup, bring this to a boil and boil for 5 minutes, stirring occasionally. Stir in the salt, vanilla and soda. Pour the sugar mixture over the popcorn and peanuts and stir this mixture until evenly coated (you should do this rather quickly, as the mixture will start to set up). Bake the mixture in the preheated oven for 1 hour, stir the pan every 15 minutes or so. Cool and store in an airtight container, do not refrigerate!

PARCHED PEANUTS

Preheat the oven to 300°. Spread about 2 cups raw peanuts on a cookie sheet and place in the preheated oven. Roast for 15 minutes. Remove from the oven and allow to cool. If you like salted peanuts,

(continued)

1

place parched peanuts in a bowl and add 2 teaspoons peanut oil, stir to coat the peanuts and salt to taste.

SEAFOOD PATE

½ lb. fresh, steam cooked tuna (chop into sm. pieces)
½ lb. fresh, steam cooked salmon (chop into sm. pieces)
½ lb. fresh, steam cooked scallops (Bay or sea)
½ lb. fresh, peeled and deveined shrimp, steam cooked

Note: the above weight is after cooking.

1 T. chopped onion
1 T. Louisiana Hot Sauce
1 tsp. chopped garlic
1 T. capers
½ tsp. salt
2 oz. heavy whipping cream

Mix together all the ingredients except for the whipping cream and separate into 2 batches. Process 1 batch at a time in a food processor, adding 1 ounce of the whipping cream to each batch while processing. Processing time will be around 2 minutes for each batch. Mix both batches together. Chill about 2 hours before serving. Makes 2 pounds.

SHRIMP PATE

2 lbs. med. fresh shrimp
2 T. lemon juice
1 tsp. Worcestershire sauce
½ c. butter, softened
1 (3-oz.) pkg. cream cheese, softened
½ c. mayonnaise (don't use the diet stuff)
2 tsp. crushed garlic
¼ c. fresh parsley
1 T. dried basil
1 tsp. dried rosemary
½ tsp. dried oregano
1 T. hot sauce

Bring about 2 quarts of water to boil in a large (4-quart) pot. Add somewhere around 1 tablespoon salt and the shrimp. Cook the shrimp just until they turn pink, 2 minutes or less. Immediately drain the shrimp and rinse with cold water, this will stop them from cooking and becoming tough. Peel the shrimp. Take half the shrimp and process in your food processor until very fine (kind of like a mush). Process the remaining shrimp into pieces about the size of a grain of corn, keep them separated and set aside. Now, combine all the rest of the ingredients until well

(continued)

27408F-99

mixed, an electric mixer will make this a whole lot easier. Mix into this the mushed up shrimp until well mixed. Add the corn kernel sized shrimp pieces and mix them in well. You will end up with about 3½ to 4 cups of pate mixture. If you have a nice 4-cup mold, coat the inside with melted butter and spoon the soft mixture into it, if not, Ramekins or cereal bowls with work just as well. Refrigerate for about 8 hours. Turn the molds up side down onto a serving plate and unmold. If you find that they do not want to come out of the mold, momentarily dip the mold into hot water and try again, do not get any water on the pate inside the mold. Serve at your next party with your favorite crackers, it is sure to be a hit.

LOBSTER CHEESE BALL

1 lb. cooked and chopped lobster
   meat*
8 oz. cream cheese, softened
1 T. fresh lemon juice
1 tsp. grated Vidalia or Bermuda
   onion
1 tsp. horseradish
½ tsp. minced garlic
1 T. capers, chopped fine
½ c. chopped pecans or walnuts
   (I prefer pecans)
3 T. finely chopped parsley

Combine all the ingredients except for the lobster meat, pecans and parsley in a mixing bowl and mix them real well. Add the lobster meat and mix well. Refrigerate for about 4 hours. Mix the pecans/walnuts with the parsley. Remove the cheese ball mixture from the refrigerator and shape into a ball. Mix the parsley and pecans together. Roll the cheese ball in the pecan parsley mixture and refrigerate until ready to use.

*Hint: You can use langinstanos, nobody but you and Chef Dirt will know the difference.

MADGES' OYSTER ROLL

2 (8-oz.) pkgs. cream cheese
2 cans smoked oysters
2 tsp. Worcestershire sauce
2 T. mayonnaise
1 garlic clove, crushed
2 T. onion, finely chopped
2 T. chopped pimentos (blot the
   pimentos dry with a paper towel
   before chopping)
½ c. chopped pecans
2 T. fresh parsley, chopped

Combine the mayonnaise, cream cheese, Worcestershire sauce, garlic, pimentos and onion. Using and electric mixer, cream until fluffy.

(continued)

27408F-99

Drain the oysters and pat them dry using paper towels. Chop the oysters and set them aside. Place a large piece of plastic in the bottom of a jelly-roll pan or baking sheet. Spread the cream cheese mixture on the plastic wrap, 1/2 inch thick. Place the pan in the refrigerator and chill for about 1 hour or until the cream cheese mixture is firm. Spread the chopped oysters on the cream cheese and roll up jelly roll fashion, removing the plastic wrap as you roll, if you don't do this, it is going to be awfully chewy. Mix together the parsley and chopped pecans. Roll the cheese roll in the pecan/parsley mixture until completely covered. Place the roll in the refrigerator and chill for 1 hour before slicing.

Madge Meyle

CABBAGE ROLLS WITH OYSTER DIPPING SAUCE

2 c. Napa or plain cabbage
2 c. shredded carrots
1 c. bean sprouts
1/2 c. chopped, dried shitaki
   mushrooms
3/4 c. chopped, fresh cilantro
1/3 c. chopped green onions
3 T. fresh, minced ginger

1 sm. cayenne red pepper,
   chopped fine, with seeds
1/4 c. rice wine vinegar
2 T. sesame oil
2 T. soy sauce
15 rice paper wrappers
Oyster Dipping Sauce

Combine all ingredients except rice paper wrappers and Oyster Sauce in a bowl, cover and refrigerate for 10 hours. Soften the rice paper wrappers in warm water for 30 to 45 seconds. Drain the vegetable mixture. Lay the rice paper wrappers on a flat surface, one at a time. Spoon about 1/4 cup of vegetable mixture in center of wrapper and roll up burrito style. Place seam side down and cover with a damp hand towel until all rolls are completed. Cut rolls in half on the diagonal, serve with the Oyster Dipping Sauce. Makes 32 appetizers.

Oyster Dipping Sauce (combine in a food processor):

1/2 c. fresh lime juice
2 tsp. fresh minced ginger
1 T. brown sugar
1 1/2 tsp. minced fresh cilantro
2 T. chopped roasted peanuts

1 T. chopped pecans (opt.)
1 tsp. minced green onion
1/4 tsp. minced garlic
1 T. oyster sauce

Process the mixture for 15 seconds on high. May be served chilled or at room temperature.

27408F-99

TARTAR SAUCE

1 c. mayonnaise
1½ T. minced sweet pickles
1½ T. minced fresh parsley

½ tsp. dried mustard
1½ T. chopped capers (opt.)
1 T. minced onion

Combine all the ingredients to mix well. Chill at least 4 hours before serving. Makes about 1¼ cups.

CRANBERRY SAUCE

4 c. fresh cranberries
2 c. water

2 c. white sugar

Cook the cranberries in water for about 10 minutes, or until all the skins pop open. Strain the cranberry mixture through a fine sieve to remove the skins and seeds. You now have the pulp and juice of the cranberry. Boil this mixture for about 4 minutes and pour into a mold, a tin can will do fine but a pretty butter mold is preferred (butter molds can still be found at some flea market sales, and are great for molding all kinds of different things. If you are lucky enough to find one, buy it!) Put the mold in the refrigerator to set the cranberry sauce. Unmold onto a serving dish by placing a hot wet towel around the mold for about 30 seconds, place the serving dish on top of the mold, then invert the mold and serving dish at the same time, lift up the mold, the cranberry sauce should remain on the dish, perfect and ready for your table. Keep chilled in the refrigerator until ready to serve. Serve with your Thanksgiving or Christmas dinner or whenever you feel festive.

BUTTER AND GARLIC CREAM SAUCE

2 sticks butter
2 lg. cloves garlic, crushed and
chopped real fine
2 T. Shake and Blend flour (this
flour is made especially for
sauces and gravies, it is put out
by Pillsbury)

¼ tsp. white pepper
¼ tsp. salt
2 c. half-and-half

Melt the butter in a medium size saucepan and add the flour, cook for one minute, stirring continuously. Remove from the heat and add the garlic, salt and pepper. Stir well and let stand for 2 minutes. Add

(continued)

27408F-99

the half-and-half and stir well, using a wire whip if you have one. Return the pan to the heat and cook until the sauce starts to thicken, about 3 minutes on medium heat. Remember to stir throughout the cooking process or the whole mess will lump on you, and you will have to start all over again. Serve over sautéed fish, shrimp or crab.

MAYONNAISE

3 tsp. dry mustard
1 T. lemon juice
1 tsp. salt
1 tsp. sugar

2 egg yolks
1³/₄ c. corn or vegetable oil
1 T. lemon juice

In a cold bowl, whip together the mustard, salt, sugar and 1 tablespoon lemon juice. Whip about 25 times using a wire whip. Whisk in egg yolks, then whisk in the oil, drop by drop until ¼ cup has been added. Continue beating in oil, slowly; when mixture is thick beat whisk in vinegar and 1 tablespoon lemon juice alternately with oil until all are used. Keep cool and use within 2 days.

CHOCOLATE GRAVY

3 T. flour
3 T. cocoa
6 to 7 T. sugar

4 c. milk
¼ tsp. vanilla
¼ tsp. salt

Mix flour, cocoa and sugar and salt together in a bowl and set aside. Heat milk to a scalding hot in a large saucepan. Add the vanilla to the hot milk. Gradually add the flour/cocoa mixture to the hot milk, stirring continuously until it thickens. Serve over hot biscuits, pancakes toast, waffles or what ever else you like.

DELLAS' CHOCOLATE SAUCE

1 c. semi-sweet chocolate pieces
²/₃ c. white corn syrup
¼ c. light cream

1 T. butter
¼ tsp. vanilla extract

(continued)

6

In a double boiler combine the chocolate and corn syrup, heat and stir until blended. Next add the cream, butter and vanilla extract, stir until well blended. Serve warm over ice cream or pound cake.

GRAVY FOR WILD GAME, DUCK AND GEESE

Drain the pan dripping from the roasting pan used for cooking game, add to this about 3 tablespoons of Roux (recipe for Roux is in this book). Mix well to blend, if you are making this gravy for duck, goose, or any other game bird, do the following; add about 2 cups water to a saucepan, add the giblets (liver, heart and gizzard), bring to a boil, then cover and reduce to a simmer, simmer for about 15 minutes. Remove the giblets from the liquid, chop up and return them back to the cooking liquid. Add the Roux mixture to the giblet mixture and cook over low heat until thickened, stirring continuously. For game animals, such as possum, raccoon, rabbit, squirel, etc., add water to the Roux mixture and cook until thickened, if your gravy is too thin, add more Roux, if it is too thick add more water. Add salt and pepper to taste.

"FIRE IN THE HOLE" SALSA

1 pair rubber gloves (this is no joke, wear them while chopping the peppers. If you don't you will be sorry later)
1 lg. habanero pepper, seeded and chopped very fine
1 lg. jalapeño pepper, seeded and chopped

1 c. fresh, seeded and chopped tomato
1 c. peeled, seeded and chopped cucumber
¼ c. chopped cilantro
½ c. sour cream

Combine all the ingredients in a bowl. Let stand at room temperature for 1 hour, then refrigerate covered until ready for use. Goes great as a garnish for grilled chicken or fish, but be very careful, it is extremely hot.

CHEF DIRT'S PEPPER JELLY

6 lg. red bell peppers
2 lg. jalapeño peppers
1½ c. vinegar, divided in half
6 c. sugar

½ tsp. salt
2 (3-oz.) pkgs. each liquid fruit pectin and melted paraffin wax

(continued)

Remove the seeds from all the peppers and chop them coarsely. Place half the chopped peppers and half the vinegar in a blender and blend until smooth, do the same with the remaining peppers and vinegar. Add this puréed mixture to a large pot and add the sugar and salt, mix well. Bring the mixture to a boil while stirring. Once it comes to a boil add the pectin. Reduce the heat to medium and continue until the mixture forms a sheet like film on a large metal spoon, this should take about 30 minutes of cooking time. Stir often about every 3 or 4 minutes. (You need to have your jelly jars sterilized and ready to go before the cooking process is completed.) Now you need to work real fast. Pour the hot jelly mixture into the sterilized jelly jars. Cover the top of the jelly with the melted paraffin wax. Cover immediately with the metal lids and screw down tight. This recipe makes 6 half pints.

HONEY BUTTER

½ c. honey
½ c. butter, softened

¼ tsp. cinnamon
¼ tsp. vanilla extract

Combine honey, butter, cinnamon and vanilla extract in mixing bowl and mix on medium speed until it is kind of light and airy. Store in an air tight container but do not refrigerate. Will keep for about 2 weeks. Serve on biscuits, toast, waffles, or pancakes, it is also great as a dip for fried chicken.

CRAB AND APPLE FRITTERS WITH ORANGE MARMALADE DIPPING SAUCE

2 c. vegetable oil
1 c. self-rising flour
8 oz. crab meat
½ c. fresh corn
½ c. peeled minced, Granny Smith apples

2 eggs, slightly beaten
1 tsp. Old Bay seasoning
¼ tsp. salt
1 tsp. sugar
¼ c. water

Pour the 2 cups of oil into a 2-quart saucepan and heat to 375°. Sauté the minced apples in 1 tablespoon of butter for 2 minutes, or until tender. Heat the oil in a 2-quart saucepan to 375°. Combine the flour, crab meat, corn, eggs, Old Bay seasoning, salt, sugar and sauté apples in a mixing bowl and mix well. Let this mixture set for about 5 minutes. Drop by rounded tablespoonfuls into hot oil. Fry until golden

(continued)

27408F-99

brown. Drain on paper towels. Makes about 30. Serve with Orange Marmalade Sauce for dipping.

**Orange Marmalade Dipping
Sauce:**

1 (10 to 12-oz.) jar orange marmalade	4 T. white vinegar
	1 T. sugar

Combine marmalade, vinegar and sugar and mix well.

DIRT'S' MINT JULEP

For one Julep:

¼ c. Jim Beam or other good bourbon	1 T. mint syrup
	Fresh mint sprigs for garnish

Mix bourbon and syrup and pour over crushed ice in a chilled glass.

Mint Julep Syrup:

1½ c. freshly chopped mint	2 c. water
2 c. sugar	

Tie the mint in a cheesecloth bag and place in a medium saucepan, add the water and sugar. Bring the mixture to a boil over medium high heat and cook until the sugar dissolves, stirring constantly. Let cool and store in the refrigerator, in a glass jar with a lid. Throw the mint bag away. Can also be used to sweeten tea, lemonade, or spoon over vanilla ice cream.

EMMAS' LEMONADE SYRUP

2 c. lemon juice	1½ c. sugar, a little more if you like it sweeter
¼ c. grated lemon rind	

Combine all ingredients and mix well; pour into a glass jar with a lid, and store in a cool place or the icebox to keep it from fermenting. **To make a glass of lemonade:** Pour ¼ cup of syrup in a tall glass, fill with water and ice and garnish with sprigs of fresh mint, if you like.

27408F-99

EMMAS' SPICED CIDER

1 tsp. whole allspice
2 sticks cinnamon about 2 inches long
12 to 14 whole cloves

2 qt. apple cider
²/₃ c. packed brown sugar
Ground nutmeg to taste

Tie the allspice, cinnamon and cloves up together in a piece of cheesecloth. In a large pot combine the cider and brown sugar and heat add the spice bag and simmer for about 10 minutes. Serve in hot mugs with ground nutmeg sprinkled over the top.

Note: My husband likes to put hard stuff in this, but don't you.

CINDY'S' COCONUT SHRIMP

30 lg. shrimp
³/₄ c. self-rising flour
2 tsp. sugar

³/₄ c. 7-Up
³/₄ c. all-purpose flour
2½ c. sweetened flaked coconut

Peel shrimp leaving the tail section on. Mix the sugar, 7-Up and self-rising flour and set aside. Coat each shrimp with the all-purpose flour, dip the shrimp, one by one into the 7-Up flour mixture and roll in the coconut. Pour 3 to 4 inches of peanut oil into a 2-quart saucepan and heat to 375. Cook 4 to 6 shrimp at a time for 1 to 2 minutes or until golden brown. Drain on paper towels.

RECIPE FAVORITES

27408F-99

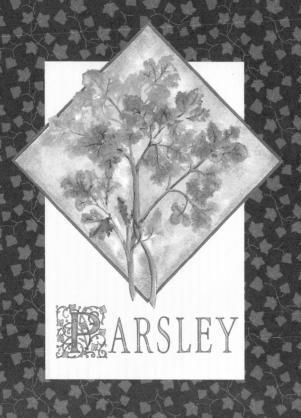

PARSLEY

Soups, Salads
& Vegetables

Helpful Hints

- Fresh lemon juice will remove onion scent from hands.

- To save money, pour all leftover vegetables and water in which they are cooked into a freezer container. When full, add tomato juice and seasoning to create a "free" soup.

- Three large stalks of celery, chopped and added to about two cups of beans (navy, brown, pinto, etc.), will make them easier to digest.

- When cooking vegetables that grow above ground, the rule of thumb is to boil them without a cover.

- A lump of sugar added to water when cooking greens helps vegetables retain their fresh color.

- Never soak vegetables after slicing; they will lose much of their nutritional value.

- Fresh vegetables require little seasoning or cooking. If the vegetable is old, dress it up with sauces or seasoning.

- To quickly bake potatoes, place them in boiling water for 10 to 15 minutes. Pierce their skins with a fork and bake in a preheated oven.

- To cut down on odors when cooking cabbage, cauliflower, etc..., add a little vinegar to the cooking water.

- To avoid tears when cutting onions, try cutting them under cold running water or briefly placing them in the freezer before cutting.

- A little vinegar or lemon juice added to potatoes before draining will make them extra white when mashed.

- To avoid toughened beans or corn, add salt midway through cooking.

- For an easy no-mess side dish, try grilling your vegetables along with your meat.

- To dress up buttered, cooked vegetables, sprinkle them with toasted sesame seeds, toasted chopped nuts, canned french-fried onions or slightly crushed seasoned croutons.

Soups, Salads & Vegetables

CRYSTALLIZED FLOWERS

2 tsp. dried egg whites (Dried egg whites can be found in health food stores, gourmet shops, and some large grocery stores.)
2 tsp. warm water

Edible flowers (Nasturtiums, lilacs, pansies, roses, violets and apple blossoms, only to mention a few.)

Combine the egg whites and water in a small bowl and mix gently with a fork for a couple of minutes until the powder absorbs the water. Beat the egg white mixture with a wire whip until foamy. Using a clean artist brush, lightly coat each flower (you may use only the petals if you like) with the egg mixture. While the flowers are still wet, sprinkle lightly with granulated sugar. Let dry on waxed paper overnight, then store in an airtight container and place in the refrigerator, can be stored up to 8 days. Use to decorate cakes, desserts, main course dishes, vegetable dishes, or arrange over salads. You wont believe your eyes!

Note: Make sure the flowers are organically grown and have not been sprayed with insecticides or other chemicals.

CHEF DIRTS' SMOKED SALMON CHOWDER

1 lb. smoked salmon, skin and bones removed
5 bacon slices
2 onions, chopped fine
2 celery stalks, diced
1 garlic clove, crushed and chopped fine

2 T. all-purpose flour
2 c. chicken broth, you can use canned
2 c. half-and-half
$\frac{1}{4}$ tsp. salt
2 T. fresh chopped parsley

Cook the bacon over medium heat until crisp. Remove the bacon and leave the drippings in the skillet. Add the garlic, celery and onions to the skillet and sauté until tender, this will take about 6 to 8 minutes. Remove the skillet from the heat for about 1 minute. Add the flour to the skillet and return to the heat, stirring continuously, cook for about 1 minute. Remove the skillet from the heat for about 2 minutes. (Now use a wire whip if you have one.) Slowly add the chicken broth to the skillet and cook for 5 minutes, stirring continuously. Empty the contents of the skillet into a 2-quart saucepan. Crumble and add the bacon to the mixture, stir. Break up and add the smoked salmon to the mixture. Place the saucepan over medium heat, add the half-and-half gradually,

(continued)

27408F-99

stirring constantly. Cook for about 8 minutes or just until it is heated through, stirring occasionally. Do not boil! Serve in bowls topped with about a teaspoon gob of butter, and garnish with fresh, chopped parsley. Makes about 6 servings.

CREAM STYLE FISH CHOWDER

¼ lb. salt pork
3 med. onions, sliced
5 med. potatoes, (if new, wash and leave skin on, if not peel), diced
3 tsp. salt
¼ tsp. black pepper

About 1½ lbs. fresh, skinless fish fillets (cod, haddock, flounder, trout, spot or croaker)
3 c. boiling water
1 qt. scalded milk
1 c. evaporated milk
3 T. butter

Cut salt pork into ½-inch cubes. Cook in a Dutch oven or large kettle until browned. Remove pork from the fat and set meat aside. Add onions to the pork fat, and cook until tender. Add potatoes, salt, pepper and water. Cover and simmer for about 20 minutes. Cut fish into bite-size pieces and add to the pot. Cook for another 5 minutes, add milk, evaporated milk and butter, heat until just hot and serve immediately with saltine or oyster crackers. Makes about 6 servings.

PEA ISLAND FISH CHOWDER

¼ lb. salt pork
3 med. onions, sliced
5 med. potatoes (if new, wash and leave skin on, if not peel), diced
3 tsp. salt
¼ tsp. black pepper

About 1½ lbs. fresh, skinless fish fillets (cod, haddock, flounder, trout, spot or croaker)
1 bay leaf
8 c. water

Cut salt pork into ½-inch cubes. Cook in a Dutch oven or large kettle until browned. Remove pork from the fat and set meat aside. Add onions to the pork fat and cook until tender. Add potatoes, salt, pepper and water. Cover and simmer for about 20 minutes. Cut fish into bite-size pieces and add to the pot. Cook for another 5 minutes. Add reserved pork and stir lightly. Serve hot with saltine crackers. Makes about 6 servings.

27408F-99

CAPE HATTERAS CLAM CHOWDER

2 c. diced potatoes
1 (32-oz.) can OR 40 top neck
    clams
½ lb. salt pork, cut into very small
    cubes, about ¼-inch
½ c. chopped celery
½ c. chopped onions
1 tsp. coarse to cracked ground
    pepper (personally I prefer
    cracked pepper)

½ tsp. salt (this may not be
    enough for you, but I suggest
    you salt to taste after cooking)
¼ tsp. thyme (if you can get
    fresh, use it; you will need to
    use about 1 tsp. chopped fresh)
1 bay leaf
6 tsp. (there or about) fresh
    parsley

Drain clams, reserving liquid. Combine clam liquid, celery, potatoes, onions, pepper, thyme, bay leaf and salt pork in a large stock pot. Make sure all of this is covered with about 3 inches of liquid, if not add water until it is. If you are using fresh clams, chop them up (not too fine, about the same as the salt pork), the canned clams will probably already be chopped. Add the clams to the stock pot and heat just until hot and serve, do not over cook or the clams will be tough. Garnish each serving with about 1 teaspoon fresh chopped parsley (if you don't have fresh parsley, don't worry, it will be good without it). Makes about 6 servings, serve with crackers or a hard, crusty bread.

MANHATTAN CLAM CHOWDER

1½ c. diced carrots
3 c. clam liquid
2 doz. shucked, raw, chowder
    clams (or top necks)
3 slices bacon, diced
1 tsp. dried thyme
1 T. fresh chopped parsley
½ tsp. dried thyme

1 c. chopped onions
3 c. peeled, cubed potatoes
½ c. diced celery
5 c. hot water
2 tsp. salt
⅛ tsp. black pepper
1 (No. 2½) can tomatoes

In a large kettle, sauté the bacon until crisp, stir in 1 teaspoon thyme and the onions, cook for about 4 minutes or just until tender, stirring continuously. Add the potatoes, celery, salt, water and pepper and simmer for 5 minutes, covered. Add the tomatoes, carrots and clam liquid, if you do not have enough to make 3 cups, add water to make up the difference. Simmer uncovered over very low heat for 1 hour. Pick over each clam to make sure there are no shell pieces stuck to them. Cut the clams into small pieces and add to the soup mixture, add

(continued)

27408F-99

the ½ teaspoon thyme and parsley. Simmer, uncovered for another 10 minutes. Serve immediately. Serves 5 to 6.

NEW ENGLAND CLAM CHOWDER

3 doz. shucked raw soft shell or
  little neck clams
Strained liquid from the shucked
  clams
2 c. water
¼ lb. diced salt pork
2 chopped med. onions
2 T. all-purpose flour

¼ tsp. celery salt
¼ tsp. pepper
2 tsp. salt
3 c. peeled, diced potatoes
3 c. scalded milk
½ tsp. salt
1 T. butter
1 T. chopped, fresh parsley (opt.)

If you are using soft-shell clams, snip off the necks. In a saucepan, place clams and liquid. Add the water and bring to a boil; remove from the heat and set aside. In a large kettle, sauté the salt pork until lightly browned. Add the onion and cook until tender, about 3 minutes. Stir in the flour, celery salt, pepper, 2 teaspoons salt, potatoes and clam liquid (do not add the clams at this time). Cover and cook for about 8 minutes or until the potatoes are tender. Add the milk, clams, ½ teaspoon salt and butter. Stir to mix well, but do not cook any longer over heat. Garnish with the chopped parsley. Serves 6.

NEPTUNE CHOWDER

This dish is a little bit of trouble, but I promise you, the reward will be worth it. Prepare the stock the day before, then it will only take you minutes to serve the finished dish.

2 med. onions, diced
3 tsp. chopped garlic
1 green bell pepper, chopped
¼ c. olive oil
2 c. dry red wine
2 c. clam juice
1 (28-oz.) can diced tomatoes
1 (8-oz.) can tomato sauce
1 bay leaf

1 T. oregano
1 T. ground black pepper
1 T. basil
1 T. sugar
1 T. crushed red pepper
¼ tsp. thyme
1 tsp. salt
Juice from one fresh lemon
10 live hard crabs

Remove the top shell and clean out the lungs and entrails. Remember the crabs at this point are not cooked and must be refrigerated at once.

(continued)

27408F-99

Its also a good idea to wear a pair of heavy gloves while tearing off the back shell, the crab is not going to be too happy about this.

20 little neck clams, wash to remove any sand or mud from the outside
1 lb. unpeeled, lg. fresh shrimp
2 lbs. skinless fish fillet (mahi-mahi, rock, haddock or any white fish) cut into 1-inch chunks

1 lb. mussels, scrub and remove beards
1 lb. sea scallops

Combine the oil, onions, bell pepper and garlic in a large stock pot and sauté until tender. Add all other ingredients except for the seafood. Cover the pot and bring to a boil, reduce heat and let simmer for 1 hour. Remove the pot from the heat and let cool, place the cooled stock in the refrigerator and leave for at least 12 hours. Crab cleaning and washing of clams and mussels should be done just prior to cooking the chowder, or at least on the same day. Remove the stock from the refrigerator and heat in a large saucepan, make sure you don't scorch it. Break the crabs in half and place them in a large stock pot and add the rest of the seafood. Pour the heated stock over the seafood, bring the pot to a boil, cover, reduce heat to simmer and cook for 8 to 10 minutes. Serve immediately with warm crusty French Bread. This is a spoon and finger meal, it is a good idea to provided bibs and plenty of napkins. Makes 8 to 10 servings.

CLEO'S MINESTRONE SOUP
(It's Hearty and Tastes Good)

1 lb. shin beef with bone
5 qt. cold water
3 T. salt
1 c. dried kidney beans
2 T. olive oil
2 cloves garlic
1 med. onion, chopped real fine
½ c. chopped parsley
½ lb. chuck beef, ground up

¼ tsp. black pepper
1 c. chopped celery
2 c. chopped cabbage
1½ c. pared and chopped carrots
3½ c. chopped tomatoes
1½ c. broken-up spaghetti
1 c. zucchini squash, sliced thin
1 c. peas

It takes a long time to make this soup, so you better start the day before. **The day before:** In a large kettle with a cover, place the shin beef with bones, salt, water and dried beans, bring to a boil. Remove from heat and skim off any scummy stuff from the surface. Cover the kettle, return to the heat and simmer for 3 hours. In the oil, sauté the

(continued)

garlic, onion, chuck meat, pepper and parsley until the onion is tender. Dig out the garlic and throw it away. Remove the bone from the kettle and cut off the meat, add the meat back to the kettle along with the onion mixture, celery, cabbage, carrots, and tomatoes. Cover and simmer until the vegetables are tender, about 20 to 25 minutes. Store in a cool place or the icebox until the next day. **The next day:** While cold, skim the fat from the soup. About 1/2 hour before serving, return the kettle to the stove and bring the soup to a boil and add the spaghetti, squash and peas, cover the kettle and cook for about 10 minutes. Should serve 8.

CRAB SOUP

4 live hard crabs
1 (16-oz.) can stewed tomatoes
1 (8-oz.) can tomato sauce
3 1/2 c. water
8 oz. crab meat (you may use any or all crab meat; i.e. backfin, lump, or claw)

1 (10-oz.) pkg. frozen mixed vegetables
2 T. minced onion
1/4 tsp. thyme
1/2 tsp. salt
1/4 tsp. black pepper

To prepare live crabs; plunge the crabs into a pot of boiling water and remove, do not cook. Remove the apron and top shell, clean the crabs and refrigerate until ready to add to the soup (use within 2 hours). Add all ingredients except for the crab meat and the cleaned hard crabs to a large pot, and bring to a boil. Reduce the heat to a simmer, cover the pot and simmer for 25 minutes, stirring occasionally. Add the crab bodies to the soup and cook an additional 10 minutes. Add the crab meat, stir lightly and remove from the heat, cover and let stand for 5 minutes. Ladle soup into 4 bowls and add one crab body to each bowl. It is proper and necessary to pick the crab bodies, using your fingers. Serve with oyster or saltine crackers. Serves 4 with 2 refills.

OYSTER BISQUE

1 doz. shucked raw oysters, drained and chopped
1 T. chopped fresh parsley
4 c. whole milk
1 T. fine chopped onions
2 stalks celery, chopped

1 bay leaf
1/3 c. melted butter
1/3 c. all-purpose flour
1 1/2 tsp. salt
1/8 tsp. pepper

(continued)

27408F-99

In a small saucepan, heat oysters to a boil and immediately remove them from the heat, set aside. Scald the milk with the onion, celery and bay leaf. Strain the milk and set aside (throw away celery, onion and bay leaf). In a large saucepan, blend the butter with the flour, salt and pepper. Slowly stir in the seasoned milk over low heat, until thickened. Add the oysters to the thickened milk. Serve hot with croutons or toast points.

Note: Substitute oysters for 1⅓ cups chopped lobster meat for a real good lobster bisque.

LOBSTER BISQUE

1 c. or ½ lb. cooked, coarse chopped, lobster meat	¼ tsp. salt
1 T. minced onion	⅛ tsp. white pepper
3 T. & 1 T. butter	1¼ c. whole milk
2 T. all-purpose flour	1 T. parsley, chopped fine
	1 pinch thyme

Melt 3 tablespoons of butter in a 1-quart saucepan, over medium heat. Add the onion and sauté for 1 minute, remove from heat. Add the flour to the butter and onion mixture and stir well. Place back over medium heat and cook for 1 minute, stirring continuously. Remove from heat and let cool for 15 minutes (you have just made the roux, roux is the base for most gravies, sauces and bisque). Add the parsley to the cooled roux and mix well, the roux will have a green tint. Add ¼ cup of milk to the roux and blend until all the roux is loose from the sides and bottom of the pan (mixture will be lumpy). Add the rest of the milk and place the pan back over medium heat. Using a wire whip, stir continually while heating and continue cooking until the mixture is bubbly and thickened. Remove from the heat and add the lobster meat and 1 tablespoon of butter. Stir gently for about 30 seconds and serve immediately. Makes about 2½ cups.

CRAB BISQUE

8 oz. lump crab meat	⅛ tsp. white pepper
1 T. minced onion	1¼ c. whole milk
3 T. & 1 T. butter	1 T. parsley, chopped fine
2 T. all-purpose flour	1 pinch thyme
¼ tsp. salt	

(continued)

27408F-99

Melt 3 tablespoons of butter in a 1-quart saucepan, over medium heat. Add the onion and sauté for 1 minute. Remove from heat. Add the flour to the butter and onion mixture and stir well. Place back over medium heat and cook for 1 minute, stirring continuously. Remove from heat and let cool for 15 minutes (you have just made the roux that will be the base for this bisque). Add the parsley to the cooled roux and mix well, the roux may take on a green tint, do not be alarmed, this is natural. Add ¼ cup of milk and blend until all the roux is loose from the sides and bottom of the pan (mixture will be lumpy, don't worry, the lumps will go away). Add the rest of the milk and place the pan back over medium heat. Using a wire whip, stir continually while heating and continue cooking until the mixture is bubbly and thickened. Remove from the heat and add 1 tablespoon butter and the crab meat. Stir gently until the crab meat is blended (try not to break up the lumps), and serve immediately. Makes about 2½ cups.

Note: If you can get them, cooked hard crab claws make a great garnish for this bisque, simply add 1 or 2 to each cup.

RUM BAKED BEANS

1 lb. dried navy beans	1½ tsp. salt
2 whole cloves	2 med. onions, chopped
1 sm. onion, left whole	2 sm. cloves garlic, chopped
½ lb. salt pork (steak of lean variety)	1 T. dry mustard
	2 T. molasses
1 sm. bay leaf	¼ c. rum

Wash and soak beans for at least 6 hours, overnight is ideal. Drain the beans and place in a large Dutch oven. Insert the cloves in the small onion. Place the onion, salt pork, bay leaf and salt in the Dutch oven with the beans. Cover the beans with about 3 inches of water and bring to a boil, reduce the heat, cover and simmer for 1 hour. Remove the Dutch oven and drain the beans, reserving the liquid. For the next step you will need 2½ cups of the drained liquid, if you don't have enough add water to it, set this aside for right now. Throw away the onion, cloves and bay leaf. Pour the beans and salt pork back into the Dutch oven. Mix the molasses, saved bean liquid, chopped onions, mustard and salt in a bowl, stir to mix well. Pour the liquid over the beans in the Dutch oven, cover and place the Dutch oven in a 350° oven. Bake for 1 hour. Remove the Dutch oven from the oven and pour the rum over the top, stir gently to combine. Replace the Dutch oven

(continued)

18

back in the oven and bake for an additional 45 minutes. Makes about 10 servings.

GRANDMA'S BAKED BEANS

1 lb. pea or navy beans
5 c. water
2 tsp. dry mustard
¼ tsp. pepper
3 med. onions, quartered

¼ c. brown sugar
¼ c. molasses
2 T. vinegar
¼ lb. salt pork, cut into ½-inch cubes

Wash and pick through beans. Cover with about 3 cups of water and soak overnight. Add 2 cups of water and all the other ingredients except for the pepper and salt pork. Cover and boil for about one hour. Place beans in a Dutch oven and add the pepper and salt pork. Cover and place in a 250° oven and bake for 6 to 8 hours. After 4 hours of baking add about ¾ cup of water or just enough to cover. Remove the cover during the last ½ hour of baking. Serves 4 to 6.

CHEF DIRT'S' FRIED OKRA

1 lb. fresh okra
½ tsp. salt
¼ tsp. Old Bay seasoning

1½ c. buttermilk
2 c. self-rising flour
Corn, vegetable or peanut oil

Wash and drain the okra. Cut off the tip and stem end. Cut the okra into 1-inch slices. Place the sliced okra in a bowl and sprinkle with salt, toss. Add the buttermilk to the bowl and let sit for 15 minutes. Drain okra well. Mix the flour and Old Bay in a plastic bag. Add the drained okra, about ⅓ pound at a time, to the bag and shake to coat. Remove the okra from the bag, shaking off the excess flour. Place the flour coated okra on a plate until ready to fry. Heat about 3 inches of oil, in a heavy pot, to 375°. Add okra, small batches at a time to the hot oil and fry until golden brown. Remove from the pot with a slotted spoon and drain on paper towels.

27408F-99

FRIED SQUASH MEDLEY

2 T. olive oil
2 T. butter
3 c. zucchini squash, sliced
3 c. yellow squash, sliced
1½ tsp. fresh chopped parsley

¼ tsp. dried basil
1 garlic clove, minced
1 lg. onion, sliced thin
¼ tsp. pepper

Heat the butter and oil in a large skillet over medium high heat. Add all the ingredients and cook until the squash is crispy tender, about 10 minutes, stirring continuously. Makes about 6 servings.

GARLIC FETTUCCINE

2 tsp. minced garlic
1 tsp. crushed red pepper
2 T. minced fresh basil
3 T. minced fresh parsley

½ c. extra virgin olive oil
6 T. grated Parmesan cheese
6 T. grated Romano cheese
16-oz. pkg. fettuccine

Cook the fettuccine according to the package instructions until al dente (this means done, but still firm), drain and set aside. Sauté the garlic in a large skillet with 2 tablespoons of the olive oil, until golden. Add the basil and parsley and cook for about 30 seconds more. Remove the skillet from the heat, add the remaining olive oil, crushed red pepper, fettuccine and cheese and toss to mix. Salt and pepper to taste. Serves 4.

SWEET POTATO PUDDING

6 med. sweet potatoes, peeled
2 eggs, beaten
¼ lb. butter
½ c. milk
⅔ c. flour

¾ c. brown sugar
½ c. chopped pecans
¼ c. orange juice
1 tsp. vanilla
6 thin orange slices

Boil potatoes until tender, drain and mash. Add eggs, butter, milk, flour, sugar, pecans, orange juice and vanilla. Put mixture in a baking pan and cover with orange slices. Bake at 350° for 30 minutes or until edges are golden brown. Serves about 6.

27408F-99

CANDIED SWEET POTATOES

6 med. sweet potatoes	¼ c. brown sugar, packed
¼ c. butter	¼ tsp. ground cloves
2 T. water	½ tsp. ground cinnamon
½ c. dark corn syrup	

Combine sugar, cloves and cinnamon and set aside. Scrub potatoes to remove dirt and cook in boiling water for 15 minutes. Cool; peel; halve lengthwise. In a cast iron skillet or shallow baking dish, place butter, water, corn syrup and brown sugar mixture; stir just until all ingredients are combined. Lay potato halves on top of mixture. Bake in a 375° oven, uncovered, for 1 hour or until tender, basting occasionally. You can cook on top of the store, on very low heat, in the skillet uncovered, basting occasionally, until well glazed. Makes 6 servings.

SOUTHERN CORN PUDDING

8 to 12 ears of fresh corn (yellow sweet or white silver queen)	1½ tsp. salt
	1½ c. light cream

Preheat your oven to 350°. With a sharp knife shave the kernels from the cob cutting lengthwise of the ears of corn. Now take the back of the knife and scrape the cobs to get the pulp. Combine the pulp with the kernels, salt and cream, mix well; pour into a greased (1½-quart) casserole dish. Now bake uncovered for 1 hour. Serve hot with butter. Makes about 4 servings.

SUGAR AND SPICE CABBAGE

1 sm. red cabbage, cut into 6 wedges with the core cut away	¼ c. water
	2 T. burgundy wine
1 sm. onion, chopped	1 T. apple cider vinegar
2 T. white sugar	4 slices bacon, cooked crisp and crumbled
¼ tsp. fresh ground nutmeg	
1 tsp. salt	1 apple, peeled, cored and chopped
1 bay leaf	

Place the cabbage wedges in a large saucepan. Add the onion, sugar, salt, bay leaf and water. Now bring this to a boil; as soon as it comes to a boil; cover the saucepan and reduce the heat to a simmer. Let simmer for about 20 minutes (do not uncover or stir). Add the

(continued)

burgundy wine, nutmeg and apple, cook for 3 more minutes or until apple is tender. Very gently remove the cabbage to a heated platter, remove the bay leaf from the liquid and bring the heat back up to a boil under the saucepan. Boil for 1 minute. Strain the liquid and spoon the apples and onions over the cabbage. Sprinkle the crumbled bacon over the cabbage. Serve hot. Makes 6 servings.

FRIED CABBAGE

3 T. bacon drippings　　　　　　**1½ tsp. salt**
½ head cabbage, coarse chopped　**½ tsp. black pepper**
1 med. onion, chopped

Heat bacon drippings in a medium to large size cast iron frying pan over medium heat. Add cabbage, onion, salt and pepper. Cover and cook for 5 minutes. Remove cover and stir. Continue to cook uncovered until tender, about 10 minutes, stirring several times. Caution, cabbage will stick to the bottom of the skillet and burn if you are not careful to scrape the bottom while frying. Serves 4.

FRENCH-FRIED POTATOES

2 lbs. potatoes　　　　　　　　**4 c. corn oil**

Several hours before serving, about 3 or 4, peel about 2 pounds of potatoes. Cut into ⅜-inch slices, then into ⅜-inch wide strips. Wash in cold water and dry thoroughly between two, clean dish towels. In a 2-quart saucepan, pour 4 cups of oil and heat to 375°. Drop about ⅓ of the potato strips into the hot oil and cook for about 6 minutes, until the potatoes are tender but not browned. Continue this until all the potatoes have been cooked. Drain on paper towels and set aside until just before meal time. Set pan of oil aside for browning later on. **Browning:** Heat oil back to 375°. Heat oven to 300°. Drop about ⅓ of the cooked potatoes back into the hot oil and cook until golden brown. Drain on paper towel lined baking pan and keep hot until all the potatoes have been browned, they will turn out extra crispy. Serve immediately. Serves 4 to 6.

27408F-99

CHEF DIRT'S' LATKES
(Grated Potato Pancakes)

6 med.-size raw potatoes	A dash of pepper
1 sm.-size onion	A dash of nutmeg (opt.)
2 eggs, slightly beaten	1 tsp. salt
3 T. all-purpose flour	½ tsp. baking powder

Peel and grate the potatoes and onion (do not cook before grating). Place the grated potatoes and onions in a bowl and let sit for 10 to 15 minutes so the liquid will rise to the top. Now pour off as much of the liquid as possible. Stir in the eggs and all the other ingredients and stir again to mix well. Heat a large heavy skillet (cast iron works best, but you may use a coated fry pan) over medium heat, and grease well, using about 1 tablespoon of bacon fat or oil. Brown on both sides and drain on paper towels. Serve hot with warm applesauce, sugar, maple syrup or sour cream. The cakes are great for breakfast or any meal. Serves about 6.

COTTAGE FRIED POTATOES

6 peeled and cooked cold potatoes	¾ tsp. salt
3 T. bacon fat	¼ tsp. pepper

Slice potatoes and mix with salt and pepper, be careful not to break up the potatoes. Heat the bacon fat in a frying pan, add the potatoes and sauté until golden brown on underside, turn and brown the other side. Do not stir while cooking. Makes 4 to 6 servings.

GREENS AND HAM HOCKS WITH DUMPLINGS

1 lb. (give or take a few ounces) smoked ham hocks	1 c. plain corn meal
2 qt. water	1 tsp. sugar
3 to 4 lbs. turnip green, with the sm. turnips if you can find them	½ tsp. salt
¼ tsp. pepper	1½ c. boiling water
	1 egg, beaten
	½ c. all-purpose flour

(continued)

Place the ham hocks in a large pot and add the water. Cover the pot and bring to a boil, reduce the heat and cook about one hour on a simmer. While the ham hocks are cooking, wash the greens real good. Cut away the large stems and chop coarse. Peel the small turnip roots (if you have them), and cut in half. Drain the greens and turnips well. Add the greens, roots and pepper to the pot with the ham hocks. Cook for about an hour or until the turnip roots are very tender. In a bowl, add the cornmeal, sugar and salt, mix well. Stir in the boiling water. Add the egg and mix well. Drop the cornmeal mixture by the tablespoonfuls onto a floured surface and roll them in the flour to coat (these are the dumplings). Place the dumplings over the hot greens and cook, covered for about 15 minutes, over medium heat, this will feed about 6 to 8 city folks, or 2 Carolina boys.

SOUTHERN STYLE COLLARD GREENS

About 5 lbs. collard greens　　**¼ tsp. pepper**
2 qt. water　　　　　　　　　**1 tsp. vinegar**
1 tsp. salt　　　　　　　　　**1 med. chopped onion**
½ tsp. sugar

Wash the collards, at least 2 times, to remove sand and any unwanted critters. Remove the large, pulpy stems from each leaf. Coarse chop the leaves; set aside. Rinse the salt pork, removing as much of the salt as you can, pat dry and cut into slices about ½ inch thick. Cook the salt pork in a large Dutch oven (if you don't have a Dutch oven any large pot will do), 8 quarts or more, until golden brown. Now add the water slowly and bring to a boil, reduce the heat and simmer, with the lid off, for about 25 minutes. Add the collards and all the other ingredients, bring to a boil. Cover the pot, reduce the heat and simmer for about an hour, stirring occasionally. You may need to add a little water, but don't add too much. Serve with Becky's Corn Muffins and Apple Cider vinegar to drizzle over the collards (if you like). Makes about 8 servings.

27408F-99

BLACK BEANS WITH SAFFRON ORZO

1 T. olive oil
1 sm. onion, chopped
1 garlic clove, chopped
1 tsp. ground cumin
2 (15-oz.) cans black beans, drained and rinsed real good
1 c. chicken broth, you may use canned
A little bit more chicken broth
2½ c. water
½ tsp. salt
A generous pinch of Saffron threads
1 c. orzo (this is a rice shaped pasta)
1 sm. zucchini squash, diced
1 c. broccoli florets (this is only the tops of the broccoli)
1 c. diced fresh green beans
½ red bell pepper, sliced thin

Heat the oil in a heavy large skillet over medium low heat. Add the onion, cover and cook for about 12 minutes or until the onion is tender. Add the garlic and cook for another 2 minutes, uncovered. Add the cumin and stir well. Add the beans and chicken broth, cook this mixture, stirring frequently, until the beans are soft and kind of creamy, this will take about 15 minutes. If the beans seem to be a little dry, add a little bit more chicken broth. Now cover, set aside and keep warm. Bring the 2½ cups of water to a boil in a heavy medium saucepan. Remove from heat and stir in the salt and saffron, cover and let stand for about 10 minutes. Return the water back to a boil and add orzo pasta. Cover and simmer over low heat until pasta is tender and all of the liquid has been absorbed, this will take about 15 minutes. Cook the green beans, zucchini squash and broccoli in a pot of boiling salt water for 3 minutes, now drain the vegetables. Add the vegetables to the pasta and toss to mix. Divide the pasta and vegetable mixture between 6 plates and top with the hot bean mixture. Garnish each plate with the sliced red pepper and serve immediately. This goes well with a loaf of hot crusty French Bread.

WILTED LETTUCE SALAD

1 head of curly leaf lettuce
6 to 8 med.-sized green onions
¼ c. hot bacon fat
¼ tsp. salt
½ tsp. sugar
2 T. vinegar

Wash and dry lettuce between two towels and break into bite-size pieces, place in a salad bowl. Slice green onions, including top and spread over the lettuce. Combine vinegar, salt and sugar and mix well. Pour vinegar mixture over the lettuce and onions and toss. Pour hot

(continued)

27408F-99

bacon fat over the tossed salad and toss again. Serve immediately. Makes 4 to 6 servings.

CHEF DIRT'S' CHICKEN SALAD

2 lbs. cooked chicken breast,
   skinned, boned and diced
16 oz. sweet salad cubes, drained
½ c. chopped onions
½ c. chopped celery

1 tsp. white pepper
½ tsp. salt
1 T. capers
¾ c. mayonnaise
3 T. diced pimentos, drained

Combine all ingredients in a large bowl and mix well using your hands. If too dry, add more mayonnaise. Makes about 3½ pounds.

CHEF DIRT'S' SMOKED OYSTER SALAD

2 pt. fresh shucked oysters
½ med.-size red bell pepper,
   sliced thin
½ med.-size green bell pepper,
   sliced thin
1 T. minced garlic
1 sm. red onion, cut in half and
   sliced very thin

1 sm. white onion, cut in half and
   sliced very thin
1 can sm. ripe olives
1 tsp. liquid smoke
2 oz. vinegar
2 oz. olive oil
1 T. salt
2 tsp. ground black pepper

Drain the oysters and using your fingers, feel through the oyster to make sure there are no pieces of shell. Place the oysters in a hot steamer and steam for 5 minutes. Remove the oysters from the steamer and place on a plate lined with paper towels. Place the plate of oysters in the refrigerator and chill for 30 minutes. Combine all of the rest of the ingredients and add the oysters. Place in the refrigerator and chill for 2 hours before serving. Makes about 4½ cups. Serves as a salad or an appetizer.

27408F-99

FOOT STOMPING AND BELLY RUBBING SHRIMP SALAD

1 lb. med. fresh shrimp	¼ tsp. coarse ground black
½ tsp. dried dill weed	pepper
½ tsp. Old Bay seasoning	Pinch of salt (this is about ⅛ tsp.)
½ c. sour cream	1 c. shell macaroni, cooked
½ c. pecan halves	2 green onions, chopped
1 T. fresh lemon juice	1 T. mayonnaise
1 tsp. Dijon mustard	½ avocado, peeled and diced

The first thing that I want to tell you is how to cook the shrimps; get a large pot of boiling water going, to which you have added about 1 tablespoon of salt. Now once the water is boiling real good, add the shrimps. Cook them no longer than 3 minutes, 2 will probably do it because you only want them to turn pink. Any long and you can use them for rubber bands. Drain the shrimps immediately and run cold water over them, don't wait until you go smoke a cigarette or get a dip of snuff, do it right now! Peel the shrimp and set by the side, don't worry about the veins, these shrimp are so small they hardly have any. Next take all the rest of the stuff in the recipe and mix it well, real well! Now mix the shrimp with all the other stuff and put it in your refrigerator, put it in a bowl first. Let it stand about 2 hours. Serve on a bed of greens (lettuce). Will make 4 servings.

A REAL SPRINGTIME SALAD

1 lb. cottage cheese	2 T. scallions
2 c. grated raw carrot	Fresh parsley
2 c. watercress	Lettuce and seasoning to taste
¾ c. dressing of choice	

Mix the cottage cheese with salt and pepper to taste, add the finely cut scallions, both green and white; if dry add a little rich milk or cream to make it smooth. Cover individual salad plates with lettuce and on the lettuce place a helping of watercress, which has been cleaned and crisped in cold water; then in the center put a large spoonful of the cheese mixture; and around the cheese; put the grated raw carrot, and

(continued)

27408F-99

on top of cheese; a spoonful of the dressing, sprinkle top with very finely chopped parsley.

Note: This is the most attractive salad, the dark green watercress, the yellow carrot and the white cheese with tiny green specks and the dressing on top.

Note: Be sure to grate the carrot on coarse grater on the down stroke only; if you do not do this, the carrot will be mushy instead of in fine shreds.

BECKY'S COLESLAW

2½ c. shredded cabbage
½ c. shredded carrot
2 c. shredded celery root (you will probably have to go to an Asian market to find this, if not use the bottom 2 inches of the celery stalks)
¼ c. sliced green onions

2 T. peanut oil
4 tsp. rice vinegar
1 T. sugar
1½ tsp. sesame oil
1 tsp. soy sauce
¼ tsp. wasabi powder OR ½ tsp. dry mustard

Combine the cabbage, carrot, celery root and green onion; toss well. Combine in a glass jar with a lid; the oil, vinegar, sugar, sesame oil, soy sauce and wasabi powder. Shake well. Pour the dressing over the cabbage mixture, toss, and refrigerate for 3 hours. Makes 4 to 6 servings.

SUNDAY COLESLAW

1 med. cabbage, shredded
1 sm. onion, grated
1 T. sugar
¾ c. mayonnaise

2 T. vinegar
1 tsp. celery seeds
1 tsp. salt

Combine sugar, mayonnaise, vinegar, celery seed and salt and mix well. Pour over cabbage and onions and toss to combine all ingredients. Make about 3 hours before serving. Serves 6 to 8.

27408F-99

JOHN GIRL POTATOES

1 lb. potatoes, peeled and minced
   (diced real fine)
1 T. minced red bell pepper
1 T. minced green bell pepper

1 T. minced onion
½ tsp. salt
¼ tsp. black pepper
2 T. cooking oil

Heat a large skillet over medium heat and add the oil. Add all of the rest of the ingredients to the hot oil. Stir to coat the ingredients with the oil. Cover and cook until the potatoes are tender, about 15 minutes. Stir about every 5 minutes of cooking time. Makes 4 servings. This is great for breakfast, serve with eggs and sausage.

RECIPE FAVORITES

27408F-99

Recipe Favorites

BASIL

Main Dishes
& Casseroles

Helpful Hints

- When preparing a casserole, make an additional batch to freeze. It makes a great emergency meal when unexpected guests arrive. Just take the casserole from the freezer and bake it in the oven.

- To keep hot oil from splattering, sprinkle a little salt or flour in the pan before frying.

- Never overcook foods that are to be frozen. Foods will finish cooking when reheated. Don't refreeze cooked thawed foods.

- A few drops of lemon juice added to simmering rice will keep the grains separated.

- Green pepper may change the flavor of frozen casseroles. Clove, garlic and pepper flavors get stronger when they are frozen, while sage, onion and salt get milder.

- Don't freeze cooked egg whites; they become tough.

- Spray your grill with vegetable oil to prevent sticking.

- Instant potatoes are a good stew thickener.

- When freezing foods, label each container with its contents and the date it was put into the freezer. Store at 0°. Always use frozen cooked foods within one to two months.

- Store dried pasta, rice (except brown rice) and whole grains in tightly covered containers in a cool, dry place. Always refrigerate brown rice, and refrigerate or freeze grains if they will not be used within five months.

- Glazed pottery, earthenware, glass, metal - all can be used for casseroles. Many of these casserole containers come in bright colors and pleasing designs to complement your tableware. The type of container you use makes very little difference, as long as it is heatproof.

- Soufflé dishes are designed with straight sides to help your soufflé climb to magnificent heights. Ramekins are good for serving individual casseroles.

- To keep boiled lasagna noodles from sticking together as they cool, keep the noodles separate by draping them over the rim of a pot.

Main Dishes & Casseroles

CORNED BEEF AND CABBAGE

4 to 6 lbs. corned beef brisket
3 to 4 thick onion slices
4 whole cloves
6 whole black pepper corns
1 bay leaf

½ tsp. rosemary
2 garlic cloves
1 T. pickling spices
1 lg. head cabbage

Place the whole piece of brisket in a large deep kettle and cover with cold water. Add the onion, cloves, pepper corns, bay leaf, rosemary, garlic cloves and pickling spices. Cover the kettle and bring to a boil, reduce the heat and simmer for about 5 hours or until fork tender. Remove the brisket from the cooking liquid. Strain the cooking liquid, saving the liquid, throw the spices away. Pour the liquid back into the kettle and skim off the fat. Place the brisket back into the pot. Quarter the cabbage and place on top of the meat. Cook at a simmer for about 20 minutes. Arrange the brisket and cabbage on a platter and serve hot. Be very careful when removing the meat from the kettle, it is very tender and may fall apart on you, if it does, don't worry it will still taste good, just wont look so pretty. This dish should serve about 6 people. If you don't thick you have enough cabbage, simply add more to the kettle.

FUGGED HARE

Cheese cloth
1 tsp. whole juniper berries
1 lg. bay leaf
2 to 3 lbs. rabbit, cut up
¼ lb. smoked bacon
2 med. carrots, scraped and
    coarse chopped
¼ c. diced onion

¼ c. celery, chopped coarse
½ c. chicken broth
¼ c. port wine
½ tsp. thyme, dried and chopped
¼ tsp. salt
¼ tsp. pepper
¼ rosemary, dried and crushed
2 T. currant jelly

Cut a small square from a piece of cheesecloth, about 4 x 4-inches. In the center, place the juniper berries and bay leaf, bunch and tie up the cheese cloth square to make a small bag, set aside. Rinse the chicken with cold water and pat dry with paper towels. In a large (4-quart) Dutch oven, add the bacon and cook over medium heat until the bacon is crisp. Remove the bacon from the Dutch oven and set aside, leave as much of the bacon fat in the Dutch oven as you can. Add the chicken to the Dutch oven and brown, do this in 2 batches. Remove the chicken

(continued)

27408F-99

and set aside. Make sure you have about 1 tablespoon fat left in the Dutch oven, if not add more to make up the difference. Add the carrots, onions and celery. Cook for about 5 minutes or until the vegetables are tender, but not brown. Add the chicken broth, wine and cheese cloth bag. Bring to a boil over high heat, scrape the bottom and the sides of the Dutch oven, remove the cheese cloth bag and throw away. Add the thyme, rosemary, saffron, salt and pepper. Return the chicken and bacon back to the Dutch oven. Put the lid on the Dutch oven, place the Dutch oven in a preheated medium high heated oven and bake for 1 hour. Remove the Dutch oven from the oven, stir in the currant jelly, salt and pepper to taste if you wish. Serves 4.

HASENPFEFFER

(Rabbit Stew)

1 (2 to 3½-lb.) dressed rabbit, cut into pieces
2 qt. cold water
1½ qt. boiling water
½ c. salt
1 c. chopped onions
2 tsp. salt

1 T. mixed pickling spices, tied up in a cheese cloth bag
½ c. vinegar
1 tsp. salt
⅛ tsp. pepper
½ c. flour
¾ c. cold water

Cover the rabbit pieces with 2 quarts cold water and ½ cup of salt, let soak for 1 hour. Drain and rinse with cold water. Place rabbit in a Dutch oven and cover with the boiling water. Add onions, 2 teaspoons salt and spice bag, cover and bring to a boil; reduce heat and simmer for 2 hours, add vinegar, cover and simmer until rabbit is tender, about ½ hour. Remove the spice bag. Add the 1 teaspoon salt and pepper. Place the flour in a skillet and brown. Stir in ¾ cup of cold water, add this to the rabbit and liquid in the Dutch oven, cook until thickened. Makes about 4 servings.

Note: Rabbit meat is practically all white, fine grained, and mild in flavor. Although pricey in the grocery store, you can probably find some-one in your area who raise rabbits for slaughter. Most of these folks will slaughter and dress the rabbit for you. If you have never had rabbit before, you owe it to yourself to venture into this great alternative to chicken.

27408F-99

ANNA'S SPARERIBS AND SAUERKRAUT

3 T. lard
3 lbs. meaty spare ribs
2 lg. onions, sliced
¼ tsp. salt
¼ tsp. black pepper
½ c. boiling water

3 c. sauerkraut
½ tsp. caraway seed
⅛ tsp. fresh ground nutmeg
1 grated cooking apple that has
    been pared and cored

Melt the lard in a large Dutch oven and sauté spare ribs on all sides until brown. Add the onions and sauté them until they are tender. Add the salt, pepper and the water and simmer covered (cook slow) for about one hour or until the ribs are tender. Next move the ribs to one side of the Dutch oven and place the sauerkraut, caraway seeds, and the apple on the other side. Cook covered, about 30 minutes. Sprinkle the ground nutmeg over the sauerkraut. **To serve:** place the spareribs on one side of the platter and cut into 6 to 8 pieces, arrange the sauerkraut and apple mixture on the other side of the platter, this should serve 4 people.

SHARON'S WHALE BONE CHICKEN

4 boneless, skinless and deboned
    chicken breasts
¼ c. butter, melted

2 c. of your favorite pasta sauce
1 c. grated Swiss cheese
1 T. chopped parsley (opt.)

Flatten chicken breast between 2 sheets of plastic wrap until about ¼ inch thick (I use a rubber mallet for this procedure, but you can use a short piece of 2 x 4, if don't have one). Then cut the flattened pieces in half. Brush each piece of chicken with the melted butter. Heat a griddle or large frying pan over medium high heat, and grill each chicken piece for 1 minute on each side and set aside. Coat a 10-inch baking dish with the pasta sauce. Layer the grilled chicken in the baking dish covering each layer with the pasta sauce (you should have 2 layers). Cover the top of the dish with the remaining pasta sauce, if you don't get an even covering of pasta sauce, simply add more sauce! It wont hurt one thing. Cover the baking dish with aluminum foil and place in a 375° oven. Bake for 30 minutes. Remove the dish from the oven, remove the aluminum foil and cover with the Swiss cheese. Place the dish, uncovered, back into the oven and cook for another 5 minutes. Garnish with fresh parsley, if desired. Serve with a green salad (a Caesar Salad would be great), and a hot, crusty loaf of garlic bread. Serves 4.

27408F-99

CHEF DIRT'S' BAKED CHICKEN AND DUMPLINGS

2½ to 3-lb. chicken, cut up
2 qt. water
1 tsp. salt
¼ tsp. pepper
½ tsp. salt
¼ c. all-purpose flour

¼ lb. butter, cut into pats (chunks)
½ c. canned milk
¼ tsp. ground sage
3 cans flaky style biscuits

Combine chicken parts (I like to include the liver and gizzard, they are my favorite parts), water and 1 teaspoon salt in a large pot for stewing. Bring the pot to a slow boil, cover and reduce to a simmer. Cook until the chicken is tender (this should take about 30 minutes). Remove the chicken from the broth, set aside and let cool. Remove about ¾ cup of broth from the stewing pot and throw away, or save for another recipe where it can be used. Now skim off most of the chicken fat from the remaining broth (you need to leave some, maybe about 3 tablespoons, more or less). Once the chicken has cooled, remove the skin and cut the meat away from the bone. Cut the meat into pieces that are bite-size, maybe a little larger and put aside for right now. Turn the heat up to about medium high under the pan with the broth in it. As the broth starts to heat add the flour, a few sprinkles at a time, stirring the whole time until all the flour has been added. Once you have added all the flour remove the pot from the heat and add the canned milk, ½ teaspoon salt, ¼ teaspoon ground sage, ¼ teaspoon black pepper, and butter pats. You have now just made your gravy (sauce). Stir the gravy well to mix all ingredients. Now be very gentle and add the cut up chicken and stir lightly to mix. Pour the chicken and gravy mixture into a 2 x 9 x 13-inch baking pan or casserole dish. Place the flaky biscuits over the top of the mixture, covering as much of the top as possible (if you have to cut some of the biscuits in half, do it). Place the pan into a preheated 375° oven and bake until the biscuits are golden brown, about 10 minutes. Serves 4.

27408F-99

FUGGED CHICKEN

Cheese cloth
1 lg. pinch saffron threads
1 tsp. whole juniper berries
1 lg. bay leaf
1 whole chicken, cut up and skin removed
2 slices bacon, coarsely chopped
2 med. carrots, scraped and coarse chopped

¼ c. diced onion
¼ c. celery, chopped coarse
½ c. chicken broth
¼ c. port wine
½ tsp. thyme, dried and chopped
¼ tsp. salt
¼ tsp. pepper
¼ rosemary, dried and crushed
2 T. red currant jelly

Cut a small square from a piece of cheesecloth, about 4 x 4-inches. In the center place the juniper berries and bay leaf, bunch and tie up the cheese cloth square to make a small bag, set aside. Rinse the chicken with cold water and pat dry with paper towels. In a large (4-quart) Dutch oven add the bacon and cook over medium heat until the bacon is crisp. Remove the bacon from the Dutch oven and set aside, leave as much of the bacon fat in the Dutch oven as you can. Add the chicken to the Dutch oven and brown, do this in 2 batches. Remove the chicken and set aside. Make sure you have about 1 tablespoon fat left in the Dutch oven, if not add vegetable oil to make up the difference. Add the carrots, onions and celery. Cook for about 5 minutes or until the vegetables are tender but not brown. Add the chicken broth, wine and cheese cloth bag. Bring to a boil over high heat, scrape the bottom and the sides of the Dutch oven, remove the cheese cloth bag and throw away. Add the thyme, rosemary, saffron, salt and pepper. Return the chicken and bacon back to the Dutch oven. Put the lid on the Dutch oven, place the Dutch oven in a preheated 350° oven and bake for 1 hour. Remove the Dutch oven from the oven, stir in the currant jelly, salt and pepper to taste, if you wish. Serves 4.

TUNA CHILI CON CARNE

2 T. peanut oil
½ c. thinly sliced onions
2 T. diced green pepper
½ lb. ground fresh tuna loin
½ c. boiling water
1 c. chopped tomatoes
1½ T. chili powder
2 T. cold water

¼ tsp. salt
¼ tsp. sugar
2 cloves garlic, minced
2 tsp. crushed red pepper
¼ tsp. wasabi powder (opt.)
2 c. canned kidney or pinto beans, with liquid

(continued)

Heat peanut oil in a skillet and cook onions and peppers until tender (about 2 minutes). Add the ground tuna; cook for 1 minute over medium high heat. Add the boiling water, tomatoes, chili powder mixed with the cold water until it is smooth and pasty, salt, sugar, garlic, red pepper and wasabi. Simmer covered for about 1 hour, uncover and simmer about 30 minutes. If the mixture gets too thick, add hot water to thin. Add the beans and heat again. Serve. This goes real well with Becky's corn muffins.

CHEF DIRT'S TUNA FETTUCCINE

4 yellow fin tuna steaks, cut about ½ inch thick*
1 (8-oz.) pkg. fettuccine pasta
6 T. butter
1 T. chopped fresh parsley
¼ c. chardonnay wine

½ tsp. salt
2 tsp. minced garlic
¼ tsp. black pepper
½ tsp. dried basil
7 oz. heavy whipping cream

Cook the fettuccine according to the package directions, drain and set aside. Melt 2 tablespoons of the butter in a large skillet, over medium heat. Add the tuna steaks to the skillet and cook for 3 minutes on each side, don't overcook, they should be medium rare. Remove the tuna to a warm plate and keep warm (not hot). Add the wine to the skillet and bring the heat up to medium high, boil until reduced by half (this is called deglazing the pan). Next add 4 tablespoons butter, the whipping cream, salt, pepper, garlic, parsley and basil. Continue cooking until the sauce is reduced by half. Remove the pan from the heat and add to it; the cooked fettuccine, toss to coat the fettuccine with the sauce. Pour the fettuccine and sauce over the tuna steaks. Serve with a warm crusty bread. Serves 4. *You can use any firm flesh white fish.

SHRIMP GUMBO

¼ c. butter
2 T. flour
2 med.-sized onions, sliced
2 cloves garlic, minced
½ green pepper, sliced thin
2½ c. tomatoes, canned or fresh
2½ c. okra, sliced, canned or fresh
⅔ c. tomato paste

3 beef bouillon cubes
4 tsp. Worcestershire
⅛ tsp. ground cloves
½ tsp. chili powder
⅛ tsp. dried basil OR ¼ tsp. fresh
1 bay leaf
½ tsp. salt
¼ tsp. black pepper
1 tsp. crushed red pepper

(continued)

27408F-99

If the little guys are going to be eating this gumbo, you may want to omit the red pepper, you can sprinkle it on individual servings.

3 c. water	3 c. hot cooked rice
1½ to 2 lbs. raw, peeled and deveined, med. or sm. shrimp	¼ c. chopped fresh parsley

Start preparing this dish at least 6 hours before serving, this allows all the ingredients to come together naturally. In a Dutch oven or heavy large skillet, melt the butter and then stir in the flour. Cook the flour and butter over low heat until brown (this makes a roux). Add the garlic, onion and green pepper, and cook slowly until tender. Add the tomatoes and rest of the ingredients except for the shrimp, rice and parsley. Simmer uncovered for about 45 minutes, cool and set aside (refrigerate if you can). About 30 minutes before serving: Cook rice and toss with the parsley, keep hot. (Try to time the cooking of the rice to coincide with the rest of the dish.) Heat the tomato mixture over medium heat until just boiling. Add the shrimp and simmer for 5 minutes. Serve the gumbo on shallow plates with the rice on the side. A nice crusty loaf of French Bread would go great with this. Serves 8.

SHRIMP GUMBO ANDOUILLE
(Ann-Do-Ey)

3 lbs. med. shrimp, peeled and deveined	1 lg. celery rib, chopped
Shrimp shells from peeled and deveined shrimp	2 T. minced garlic
	1¼ c. oil, vegetable or corn
5 qt. water	1 T. salt
4 chicken thighs	1½ c. all-purpose flour
6 bay leaves	1 cayenne pepper, chopped with seeds
¼ c. coarsely chopped parsley	1 tsp. black pepper
3 crushed garlic cloves	5 green onions, chopped
1 lb. andouille or smoked sausage, sliced	½ c. chopped fresh parsley
2 med. onions, chopped	½ tsp. file powder
1 lg. bell pepper, chopped	Hot cooked rice

Combine water, chicken, bay leaves, cilantro and shrimp shells in a large stockpot and bring to a boil. Cover, reduce heat and simmer for 1 hour. Remove the chicken, remove the skin and bone and coarsely chop the chicken. Strain off the broth and throw away the solids. Return all but 1 cup broth back to the pot and add sausage, onions, bell pepper, celery and garlic. Bring to a simmer and cook for about 1 hour, stirring

(continued)

occasionally. Heat the oil in a large heavy skillet over medium heat. Gradually whisk in the flour and cook until mixture is a dark caramel color, continue whisking while cooking (this is very important, don't stop whisking for any reason, if you do it will burn and you will have to start all over again). Whisk this mixture into the sausage and chicken mixture, bring to a simmer and cook for 1 hour, stirring occasionally. Stir in black pepper, chicken and chopped cayenne pepper; continue to cook for about 35 minutes. skim off most of the fat. Stir in the green onions and parsley, continue cooking for another 5 minutes, add the shrimp and cook for 10 minutes or just until the shrimp turns pink. Thin as desired using the cup of reserved stock. Serve over hot cooked rice.

CURRITUCK SEAFOOD GUMBO

4 slices bacon	10 to 12 fresh okra pods, sliced
¾ c. all-purpose flour	½ c. diced green onions
1 tsp. salt	8 bay leaves, finely crushed
1 tsp. black pepper	¼ tsp. minced fresh garlic
1½ c. chopped onions	2 qt. water
1½ c. diced celery	10 whole crabs, cooked and
4 c. fresh chopped tomatoes OR 2	cleaned
(16-oz.) cans tomatoes,	1 lb. fresh crab meat
undrained	1 lb. med. fresh shrimp, peeled
4 lg. jalapeño peppers, seeded	1 tsp. gumbo file
and chopped	1 lb. polish sausage, sliced

Fry the bacon in a large heavy skillet, remove, crumble and set aside. Leave the bacon drippings in the skillet. While heating the drippings over high heat, add the flour, salt and pepper, stirring continuously. Cook until the mixture is thick, pasty and golden brown (this will make the base for a roux). Reduce heat to medium and add the onions and celery, cook for another 10 minutes, stirring occasionally. Now dump all of this into a large pot and add the tomatoes, jalapeño peppers, garlic, okra, green onions, crushed bay leaves, and water. Stir real well to mix all the ingredients. Bring the pot to a boil while stirring, reduce the heat to a simmer, cover and let cook for about 2½ hours, stirring every now and then. Add the sausage, gumbo file and crabs and cook for 5 more minutes. Add the shrimp and crab meat and cook for 5 more minutes. Serve immediately over hot rice. Garlic bread would go great with this dish. Will make about 2½ quarts of the best gumbo you have ever ate.

27408F-99

NORTH OF THE BORDER PAELLA

1 lb. andouille sausage links (this is a Creole sausage, if you cannot find it you may use a hot Italian Sausage)

½ c. olive oil

2-lb. chicken, cut up

1-lb. pork loin, cut into 1-inch cubes

2 c. chopped onions

2 cloves garlic, crushed

2 c. uncooked regular rice

1 tsp. salt

1 tsp. dried oregano

½ tsp. crushed saffron threads

¼ tsp. white pepper (you may use black pepper)

3 med. peeled, seeded and chopped tomatoes

2 (10¾-oz.) cans clear chicken broth

1 lg. bay leaf

1½ lbs. med. to lg. shrimp, peeled and deveined

¾ c. frozen or fresh peas (fresh is better)

1 T. fresh chopped cilantro

Cut the sausage links in half, crosswise and brown in a large skillet. Blot the sausage with paper towels and place them in a 4½-quart shallow baking dish. Heat the olive oil in a skillet, add the chicken and brown on both sides. Do this over medium to medium high heat. Remove the chicken from the skillet and add it to the baking dish. Now add the pork to the same skillet and add cook until browned, turn often. Remove the pork from the skillet and add this also to the baking dish. Now add the onion and garlic to the same skillet and sauté over medium heat until tender, about 2½ to 3 minutes. Add to the onions in the skillet; the rice, saffron, salt, oregano and pepper. Cook over medium heat for about 10 minutes, stirring occasionally. Now, add the tomatoes, chicken broth, cilantro and bay leaf to the skillet and just bring to a boil. Remove the skillet from the heat. Spoon the mixture in the skillet over the meat in the baking dish. Cover the baking dish tightly with aluminum foil and place it in a 350° oven and bake it for 1 hour. After you have baked it for one hour, remove it from the oven. Uncover and place the shrimp and peas on top of the rice mixture, cover again and bake for another 15 minutes, if you can find it, remove the bay leaf (if you cant, be sure and tell your guest not to eat it, if they do). This dish makes about 10 servings and should be served with a hot loaf of Cuban or a crusty loaf French Bread.

Note: Every one is going to want this recipe, don't you give it to them. Tell them to buy my book!!

27408F-99

CHEF DIRT'S' SHRIMP CROQUETS

2 c. peeled and deveined and
   chopped raw shrimp
1¾ c. unsalted cracker crumbs
3 T. butter
1 T. chopped fresh parsley
1 c. milk
¼ c. all-purpose flour
1 T. minced onion
1 tsp. Worcestershire sauce

½ tsp. salt
½ tsp. black pepper
1 T. mayonnaise
1 egg, lightly beaten
2 eggs, lightly beaten
Corn or vegetable oil
1 tsp. Tabasco or any other hot
   sauce

Melt the butter in a large saucepan over low heat. Gradually add the flour whisking or stirring at the same time, cook for 1 minute while stirring. Turn heat up to medium and gradually whisk in the milk. Cook until thickened. Stir in the onion, salt, pepper, Worcestershire sauce and Tabasco sauce. Remove the saucepan from the heat and add 1 egg, the mayonnaise, shrimp and parsley chill in the refrigerator for about 1 hour. Shape the mixture into 14 balls. Beat 2 eggs lightly. Roll the balls in the beaten eggs and roll in the cracker crumbs. Flatten the balls slightly to make a rounded cake. Pour about 3 inches of oil into a large, heavy, fry pan and heat to about 350°. Fry the croquets for about 4 minutes or until golden brown. Drain on paper towels and serve with the Tartar Sauce recipe in this book, or a hollandaise sauce. Makes 6 to 7 servings.

RECIPE FAVORITES

27408F-99

Thyme

Meat, Poultry & Seafood

Helpful Hints

- Use little oil when preparing sauces and marinades for red meats. Fat from the meat will render out during cooking and will provide plenty of flavor. Certain meats, like ribs, pot roast, sausage and others, can be parboiled before grilling to reduce the fat content.

- When shopping for red meats, buy the leanest cuts you can find. Fat will show up as an opaque white coating, or can also run through the meat fibers, as marbling. Although most of the fat (the white coating) can be trimmed away, there isn't much that can be done about the marbling. Stay away from well marbled cuts of meat.

- Home from work late with no time for marinating meat? Pound meat lightly with a mallet or rolling pin, pierce with a fork, sprinkle lightly with meat tenderizer and add marinade. Refrigerate for about 20 minutes and you'll have succulent, tender meat.

- Marinating is a cinch if you use a plastic bag. The meat stays in the marinade and it's easy to turn and rearrange. Cleanup is easy; just toss the bag.

- It's easier to thinly slice meat if it's partially frozen.

- Tomatoes added to roasts will help to naturally tenderize them. Tomatoes contain an acid that works well to break down meats.

- Whenever possible, cut meats across the grain; they will be easier to eat and have a better appearance.

- When frying meat, sprinkle paprika over it to turn it golden brown.

- Thaw all meats in the refrigerator for maximum safety.

- Refrigerate poultry promptly after purchasing. Keep it in the coldest section of your refrigerator for up to two days. Freeze poultry for longer storage. Never leave poultry at room temperature for more than two hours.

- If you're microwaving skinned chicken, cover the baking dish with vented clear plastic wrap to keep the chicken moist.

- Lemon juice rubbed on fish before cooking will enhance the flavor and help maintain a good color.

- Scaling a fish is easier if vinegar is rubbed on the scales first.

Meat, Poultry & Seafood

CHEF DIRT'S' THIGHS

¼ c. olive oil
1 T. Chinese hot mustard
3 T. lime juice
3 T. lemon juice
½ tsp. sesame oil

½ tsp. pepper
1 tsp. tarragon
2 garlic cloves, minced
6 to 8 chicken thighs, skin removed

Combine all ingredients in a large bowl and mix well. Add the chicken thighs one at a time, coating each piece well with the marinade, cover the bowl tightly with a lid or plastic wrap, place the bowl in the refrigerator and let sit for 1 hour. Start preparing the grill for medium hot heat. Remove the chicken from the marinade and throw away the marinade. Place the chicken on the grill and cover with the grill lid. Grill the chicken, turning often. Be careful not to burn my thighs! Total cooking time should be around 25 minutes.

SUGAR BRITCHES CHICKEN AND CHEESE BURRITOS WITH SALSA

½ lb. boneless, uncooked, skinless chicken breast, cut into 1-inch wide strips
3 tsp. olive oil
2 garlic cloves, minced fine
½ of a small onion, minced

1 (15-oz.) can pinto beans, drained and rinsed
¼ tsp. Tabasco sauce
1 c. shredded Monterey Jack cheese
4 (10-inch) flour tortillas

Salsa:

1 c. diced fresh tomatoes
½ c. peeled, seeded and diced cucumbers
¼ c. diced red onion

2 T. chopped fresh cilantro
1 jalapeño pepper, seeded and minced

Combine the tomatoes, cucumbers, red onion, cilantro and jalapeño pepper in a bowl and set aside. Combine the chicken, 2 teaspoons olive oil and 1 garlic clove in a bowl, refrigerate for 1 hour. Heat a heavy, large no-stick skillet over high heat. Add the chicken mixture and cook for about 4 minutes, transfer the chicken to a plate and set aside. Heat the remaining 1 teaspoon olive oil in the same skillet over medium low heat; add the onion and cook until the onion is very tender, stirring continuously (cook for about 8 minutes). Stir in the remaining garlic

(continued)

27408F-99

clove and sauté for one minute, mix in the beans and remove from the heat, add the Tabasco. Preheat your oven to 350°. Spoon ¼ of bean and chicken mixture down center of 1 tortilla. Top filling with 2 tablespoons of the salsa you made up and set aside. Roll up the burrito. Place burritos in a 9 x 13-inch baking dish, seam side down, repeat this with the remaining tortillas. Sprinkle the cheese over the burritos, cover with aluminum foil and bake for 15 minutes. Serve with remaining salsa.

FRAMED EGGS

1 slice loaf bread about ½ inch thick	**1 egg** **Butter**

Heat a griddle or frying pan as you would to fry eggs. Brush both sides of bread slice with melted butter. Using a 2½-inch biscuit cutter, cut out the center of the bread slice. Place the bread slice in the center of the griddle and the cut out piece in the corner. Toast the bottom side until golden and turn over both pieces of bread. Drop about 1 tablespoon of butter in the cut out of the bread slice. Break one egg and drop into the cut out, and cook until desired doneness. Remove framed egg to plate and serve with the cut out toast circle. Makes one egg serving.

SUGAR BRITCHES SPICY BARBECUED PORK SANDWICH

12 to 16-oz. pork tenderloin	**2 tsp. minced garlic**
¼ c. water	**1½ grated fresh ginger**
¼ c. soy sauce	**½ tsp. sesame oil**
¼ c. brown sugar, packed	**4 lg. soft rolls, split**
2 tsp. red curry paste OR 1 tsp. horseradish	

Combine water, soy sauce, brown sugar, curry paste, grated ginger, sesame oil and garlic, this makes the marinade. Place the pork tenderloin in a large, plastic Ziploc bag and set in a shallow dish, pour the marinade over the pork tenderloin. Squeeze out as much air from the bag as you can, and seal, refrigerate for 8 to 10 hours or overnight, turning the bag over once and a while. Drain the tenderloin on a rack in a baking pan and cover with foil. Roast in a 425° oven for 20 minutes, uncover and roast 15 minutes more. Allow to cool and slice very thin

(continued)

27408F-99

(bias-slice). Cover and store in the refrigerator for about 24 hours. After 24 hours bring the reserved marinade to a boil. Add the sliced tenderloin and bring back to a very slow boil. Remove from the heat and let stand for 5 minutes. Remove the tenderloin slices from the marinade and arrange on split rolls. Top with Thai Coleslaw, if desired. Makes 4 servings.

COUNTRY FRIED STEAK

³/₄ c. + ¹/₄ c. + 2 T. flour
¹/₂ tsp. + ¹/₄ tsp. salt
¹/₂ tsp. + ¹/₂ tsp. pepper
¹/₈ tsp. garlic powder

3 T. bacon drippings
2 c. milk
1 lb. sirloin or round steak

Mix together in a shallow dish, ³/₄ cup flour, ¹/₂ teaspoon pepper, ¹/₂ teaspoon salt and garlic; set aside. Cut steak into 4 pieces. Using ¹/₄ cup of flour, sprinkle each piece with some of the flour on both sides. Using a meat mallet, pound both sides of each piece until it looks like, if you hit it one more time, it will fall apart. Heat the 3 tablespoons bacon dripping in a large heavy frying pan. Dredge each piece of steak in the flour mixture and place in the hot frying pan and cook over medium heat for 4 to 5 minutes or until brown, turning once. Reduce heat to low, cover, reduce heat to low and cook for 15 minutes. Uncover, raise heat to medium low to medium, cook until crisp, turning once. Remove steak and drain on paper towels, place on serving platter. Heat the drippings in the skillet and whisk in 2 tablespoons of flour over medium heat. Cook until browned, whisking constantly, until browned. Gradually add milk, whisking constantly. Cook 3 to 5 minutes until thickened. Stir in ¹/₄ teaspoon salt and ¹/₂ teaspoon pepper. Serve gravy on the side with the steak, to be spooned over the steak and/or mashed potatoes. Serve with mashed potatoes, peas and hot biscuits. Makes 4 servings. Be sure to sop those biscuits in the gravy; Yum, Yum, Yum.

KIDS LOVE BEANS AND FRANKS

2 (16-oz.) cans of your favorite
  pork & beans
1 (1-lb.) pkg. all beef hot dogs
¹/₄ c. chopped Vidalia or Bermuda
  onion

¹/₄ c. chopped green onion
¹/₂ c. catsup
¹/₂ c. corn syrup, light or dark (I
  prefer the dark)
2 T. brown sugar

(continued)

Cut the hot dogs into ½-inch pieces and combine with all the other ingredients, stir well. Spoon the mixture into a lightly greased (8-inch square) baking dish. Bake uncovered in a 350° oven for 1 hour. Makes 4 to 6 servings.

Note: Big kids like em too.

SEAFOOD BREADER MIX

2 c. all-purpose flour
½ c. plain cornmeal
1 tsp. ground cayenne pepper (leave out if you don't want the breader spicy)
½ tsp. garlic powder (reduce to ¼ teaspoon if you don't want the breader spicy)
½ tsp. onion powder (reduce to ¼ teaspoon if you don't want the breader spicy)
1 tsp. salt
1 tsp. curry powder
½ tsp. thyme
½ tsp. black pepper

Combine all ingredients in a Ziploc bag and store until ready for use. To use; pour about a cup full into a plastic bag, shake excess liquid from the fish, shrimp, etc. Coat 2 or 3 pieces at a time, adding more breader as needed.

Note: All your seafood will have a milder flavor if allowed to marinate in milk for about ½ hour before breading and frying, you can use whole or skim milk.

TWICE BREADED DEEP FRIED OYSTERS

1 pt. select oysters
2 c. seafood breader mix
2 c. peanut oil

Drain the oysters. Place 1 cup of the Seafood Breader mix into a plastic bag. Drop the oysters, 1 or 2 at a time into the plastic bag and shake until coated. Place each coated oyster on a plate and store in the refrigerator for 15 minutes. Pour the peanut oil into a 2-quart saucepan and heat to 375°. Remove the plate of oysters from the refrigerator and using the other cup of breader mix, coat again as you did before. Cook the oysters in the hot oil, 4 to 6 at a time, until golden brown, they should cook in about 1 minute. Drain the cooked oysters on paper towels and serve hot. Makes 2 servings.

27408F-99

DEEP FRIED, BEER BATTER FISH

2 lbs. skinless fish fillets

This will work with most any type of fish, a few types are: bass, catfish, bream, perch, rock, halibut, red snapper, flounder, trout...if you are using large fish such as mahi-mahi, tuna or shark cut into chunks.

1 c. self-rising flour
1 c. all-purpose flour
1 c. beer
Milk, whole or skim, it doesn't
make any difference

Oil, peanut or corn oil (I like to
use peanut oil)

Remove the skin from the fillets, using a very sharp knife, by placing the fillet skin side down on a flat surface and run the knife lengthwise between the meat and skin, if you purchase your fish from a seafood market they should be able to do this for you. Pour about 2 cups of milk into a large bowl and add the fish

Note: I cut the fish into pieces about 2 inches long, it makes things a whole lot easier.) Place the bowl in the refrigerator until ready to use, or for 30 minutes. Place about 2 inches of oil in a 2-quart saucepan and heat to 375°. Mix the self-rising flour and beer together to make the beer batter. Remove the fish from the milk and shake the excess milk off the fish. Lightly coat each piece of fish with the all-purpose flour and dip into the batter. Carefully drop the fish pieces into the hot oil, a few at a time (about 4 or 5), remember now, keep your oil hot. Remove the fish from the hot oil and drain on paper towels. Cooking time should be from 1 to 2 minutes, depending on the thickness of the fish pieces. **Serve with:** coleslaw, baked beans and hush puppies. Serves 4.

Note: You are probably wondering why you should soak the fish in milk? Answer; fish has a natural bacteria that grows on it all the time. Washing it alone will do little to remove it. This bacteria, although harmless to you will affect the taste of the fish, the enzymes in the milk will neutralize this bacteria. I do this to all my fish, no matter how I am going to prepare it.

27408F-99

CAPT. TOMMY'S STUFFED AND BAKED ROCK FISH

2 (³/₄-lb.) rock fish fillets
1 sm. onion, chopped
¼ c. butter, melted
1 T. butter
1 c. soft bread crumbs
1 T. fresh parsley, chopped
1 tsp. fresh squeezed lemon juice
¼ tsp. salt
½ tsp. coarse ground black pepper
4 slices fresh tomatoes
¼ tsp. ground thyme
4 slices bacon
2 c. fresh milk (whole or skimmed, it doesn't matter)

Place the fish fillets in a bowl, cover with the milk and place in the refrigerator for at least 30 minutes. Remove the fish fillets from the milk and rinse off with cold water, pat dry and rub each fillet with the thyme. Set aside in the refrigerator. Combine the 1 cup bread crumbs, ¼ cup butter, onion, parsley, lemon juice, salt and pepper. Stir this mixture well to mix all the ingredients. Lightly grease a 9 x 13-inch baking dish with butter. Place 2 of the fillets in the dish skin side down in the baking dish. Place the bread stuffing down the center of both fillets. Top the dressing with the other 2 fillets, skin side up. Place 2 slices of bacon on each of the 2 top fillets, top with the tomato slices, and sprinkle with the remaining bread crumbs. Bake in a 350° oven for 40 minutes or until fish starts to flake. This will make 4 servings.

RED SNAPPER SEVICHE

(Not to be confused with Sushi or Sashimi)

The fish in this recipe will appear to be cooked to every one, only you and those with a very trained eye will know otherwise. It is perfectly safe and delicious to eat or Chef Dirt would not have it in his book. Have fun with it.

1 lb. skinless red snapper fillet (This is 1 lb. after the skin has been removed)
1 c. fresh squeezed lime juice (Use only fresh squeezed)
2 ripe tomatoes that have been seeded and diced
¼ c. sliced green onions
¼ c. diced red bell pepper
2 lg. jalapeño peppers, seeded and chopped
2 T. fresh chopped cilantro
About 16 ripe olives
½ c. fresh pineapple chunks (you can use canned, just make sure you drain and blot them real well, it wont be as good though)
Bib lettuce

(continued)

27408F-99

When you purchase your red snapper fillets ask to smell it, don't worry most reputable seafood markets are proud of their fresh product and will gladly accommodate you. The fish should have a clean pleasant odor. Cut the fillets into ½-inch chunks. Arrange the fish in single layer in a large casserole dish. Mix together all the other ingredients except for the ripe olives and the pineapple chunks, stir all of this well and pour over the fish chunks, cover, place in the refrigerator and let sit for 6 to 8 hours. Remove from the refrigerator and place in salad bowls over a bed of the bib lettuce, garnish with the ripe olives and pineapple chunks. Serves 4 to 6.

BAKED TROUT SUGAR BRITCHES

2 lbs. grey or speckled trout	¼ c. chardonnay wine
1 c. lime juice	¼ c. sherry
1 c. all-purpose flour	1 T. minced green onion tops
1 (1-oz.) pkg. hollandaise sauce mix	1 tsp. fresh chopped parsley
1 tsp. garlic powder	½ tsp. minced fresh garlic
1 tsp. onion powder	½ lb. backfin crab meat
¼ c. melted butter	½ c. sliced fresh mushrooms
⅔ c. water	¼ c. toasted silvered almonds

Wash and place the trout fillets in a shallow bowl and cover with the 1 cup of lime juice. Cover and place in the refrigerator for 2 hours. Remove and drain, throw away the liquid. Combine flour, onion powder and garlic powder. Dredge the fish in the flour mixture. Heat the butter in a large skillet over medium high heat and brown the trout fillets on both sides, about 2 minutes on each side. Remove the fillets from the skillet and set aside. Pour the wine into the hot skillet and reduce to about half the liquid to deglaze the pan. Add the water, parsley, green onion tops, parsley, fresh garlic and packaged hollandaise sauce mix. Cook over low heat until thickened, stirring constantly. This will take 3 or 4 minutes cooking time to thicken. Stir in the crab meat, almonds and mushrooms. Place the trout fillets in a lightly buttered baking dish, about 2 x 9 x 13 inches. Spoon the crab mixture over the fillets cover with aluminum foil and bake in a 350° oven for 20 minutes. Serves 6 to 8.

TUNA MIGNON

**4 yellow fin tuna steaks, cut ½ to
¾-inch thick (steaks should be
a pretty red color, not brown)**

**4 T. cracked black pepper
4 T. vegetable oil**

Heat a large fry pan over medium high heat. Rub each steak with the vegetable oil and coat each steak with 1 tablespoon of cracked black pepper. Sear the steaks in the hot fry pan for 15 seconds on each side (yes, this is right, 15 seconds). Serve immediately on a warmed plate, with baked potato or garlic fettuccine. Makes four servings.

TUNA DIANE

**1 kiwi fruit
1 banana
1 star fruit (if not available,
substitute with one of your
favorite fruits)
1 mango**

**3 T. cocoa Lopez
1 T. soy sauce
2 tuna steaks, about ½ inch thick
3 to 4 bamboo skewers (soak in
water for 15 minutes)**

Heat the grill to a medium hot temperature or raise the cooking grid to about 6 inches from the hot coals. Slice the mango (you will probably do better to just cut into chunks but be sure and peel off the tough outside first, peel). Slice the star fruit (don't even think about peeling this one). Peel and slice the kiwi fruit. Cut the banana into chunks about ¾ inches long (you would be surprised at the number of people that would leave the peel on, take the peel off). Place the sliced fruit on the skewers, first a slice of mango, a slice of banana, a slice of star fruit, and a chunk of mango. Continue until you have all the fruit on the skewers (now don't they look pretty). Now, combine the cocoa Lopez and the soy sauce and mix well. This makes your basting sauce. Baste the fruit skewers and tuna steaks with the basting sauce. Place the kabobs (fruit) and the tuna steaks on the hot grill at the same time. Cook the kabobs and the tuna steaks about 3 minutes on each side (pretend the kabobs have only 2 sides). Baste 1 to 2 times on each side while cooking. Serve with the tuna steaks in the center of the plate with the fruit arranged around them (remove the fruit from the skewers first).

Diane DeVaughn Stokes

27408F-99

CHEF DIRT'S' SALMON CAKES

1 lb. fresh salmon, skin and
  bones removed
2 eggs, beaten
2 T. instant potato flakes
1 T. mayonnaise

½ tsp. Worcestershire sauce
½ tsp. salt
¼ tsp. black pepper
⅓ c. chopped onion
Peanut oil

Heat a small skillet over medium heat, add 1 tablespoon of peanut oil and sauté the onions until they are just tender, about 2 minutes or less. Remove from heat and set aside. Pour 2 cups of water into a large, heavy skillet and bring to a slow boil, add the salmon, reduce the heat and simmer for about 10 minutes. Remove the salmon from the water and drain on paper towels until completely cool. Blot the cooked salmon well with paper towels to remove any excess water or oil. Crumble the cooked and cooled salmon in a medium-sized bowl, add the instant potatoes, sautéed onions, salt and pepper and toss. In a small bowl, combine the eggs, mayonnaise and Worcestershire sauce and beat well (by hand) to combine all ingredients. Pour the egg mixture into the salmon mixture, using your hands, mix all ingredients well. Let sit for 10 minutes. If mixture is too dry add more egg, if it is too wet, add more instant potatoes (mixture should have a consistency like thick mashed potatoes). Shape into 4 patties. Heat 1 tablespoon peanut oil in a non-stick frying pan over medium heat and cook the salmon patties to a golden brown on each side, about 3 minutes on each side should do it. Serve hot as a main course or as burgers with your favorite toppings.

POACHED SALMON

¼ c. carrots, sliced thin
¼ c. yellow onions, sliced thin
¼ c. celery, sliced thin
2 T. chopped cilantro

½ tsp. salt
½ tsp. white pepper
2 c. chardonnay wine
2 (8 oz.) salmon steaks or fillets

Combine all ingredients, except salmon, in a large heavy skillet and bring to a boil. Add the salmon to the boiling mixture and reduce the heat to medium. Cook the salmon for 3 minutes, turn and cook for 4 more minutes, salmon should be pink in the center, if you want it more done, cook for an additional 2 minutes. Remove the salmon to serving plates and serve immediately. You may eat the poached vegetables, but most will find them a little too pungent. Serves 2.

27408F-99

SALMON WITH PASTA IN WINE AND CREAM SAUCE

4 (6 to 8-oz.) salmon fillets
½ c. white wine*
½ c. heavy cream
¼ tsp. white pepper
1 T. capers (opt.)

¼ tsp. salt
1 T. chopped fresh parsley
3 T. butter
2 T. oil, peanut, corn or canola
1 (16-oz.) pkg. angel hair pasta

Cook pasta according to directions on the package and arrange on a serving platter, set aside and keep warm. Heat a 10-inch or larger frying pan over medium heat. Add the oil and then the butter; add the salmon to the hot oiled pan skin side up. Cook for 4 minutes, turn and cook for an additional 4 minutes. Remove salmon to a warm plate and set aside. Deglaze the pan with the wine and continue to cook until reduced by half. Add the salt, pepper, parsley and capers. Cook for 30 seconds, add the milk and 2 tablespoons of butter. Very gently add the salmon back to the frying pan and sauce. Cook for 1 minute. Remove salmon from the sauce onto the platter of angle hair pasta and pour the sauce over the salmon and pasta. Serve immediately with a hot loaf of crust bread. Serves 4. *Use the wine you like to drink, never cook with a wine you would not drink.

BRAISED SWORDFISH WITH TOMATOES AND BASIL

2 T. olive oil
4 (8-oz.) swordfish steaks
½ c. chopped fresh basil
⅓ c. minced onions
1 garlic clove, minced
⅓ c. chardonnay wine (I prefer Chardonnay but any good white wine will do)

⅓ c. canned chicken broth (low salt)
1 c. canned chopped tomatoes with their juice
2 T. whipping cream

Heat the olive oil in a large skillet over medium high heat. Season each steak on both sides with salt and pepper. Place the steaks in the heated skillet and cook for one minute on each side. Reduce the heat to low and sprinkle the basil, onion and garlic over the fish. Cover the skillet tightly with aluminum foil and then a lid. Cook for 8 minutes. Move the steaks to a platter and set aside. In the same skillet you used to cook the steaks, add the wine and allow it to boil for about 3 minutes or until you only have about a tablespoon of liquid left, now add the

(continued)

chicken broth and allow to boil until it is reduced to about half of what you started with, about 2 to 3 minutes. Stir in the tomatoes and continue to cook until the sauce thickens. Now stir in the cream and mix well, season with salt and pepper to taste. Spoon the sauce over the steaks in the platter and serve immediately.

CLEO'S HANGTOWN FRY

(Some poor fellow got hanged so he could eat this)

8 thin slices of smoked bacon	1/8 tsp. pepper
2 T. water	1 doz. shucked oysters, drained
5 eggs	1/2 c. dried bread crumbs
1/4 tsp. salt	1/4 c. bacon fat

Fry the bacon in a skillet until crisp and drain on a clean dishtowel, and crumble. Beat the eggs with the water, salt and pepper. Dip the oysters into the egg mixture and roll in the bread crumbs. Quickly brown the oysters in the hot bacon fat, turning once. Top the oysters with the bacon (right in the frying pan); pour the rest of the egg mixture over the whole thing. Cook without turning until firm and brown on the bottom, then turn out onto a warm plate and serve hot. Should make 4 servings.

OLD HAMPTON OYSTER PIE

1/4 c. chopped green pepper	1/2 c. sliced fresh mushrooms
1 c. chopped green onions	1/4 c. all-purpose flour
1/4 c. chopped celery	1 pt. oysters (standard will do)
1 lg. garlic clove, minced	1 T. chopped fresh parsley
6 slices bacon	1 T. fresh squeezed lemon juice
1/2 tsp. salt	1 recipe of Puff Pastry mix (recipe
1/4 tsp. cayenne pepper	is in this book)

Using a large skillet, cook the bacon until crisp. Remove the bacon, crumble and set aside. Leave the bacon grease in the skillet and add the mushrooms, garlic, onions, celery, green pepper, and garlic. Sauté over medium heat until the vegetables are tender, about 4 or 5 minutes. Stir continuously while sautéing the vegetables. Add the flour, salt and cayenne pepper, stir well to mix. Stir in the oysters, bacon, lemon juice and parsley and remove from the heat. Lightly grease a 9-inch baking pan and spoon the oyster mixture into it. Layer the Puff Pastry dough

(continued)

over the top of the mixture in the baking pan. Bake at 400° for 15 to 20 minutes or until the crust is golden brown. Makes 4 to 6 servings.

SUGAR BRITCHES IMPERIAL OYSTERS

20 lg. oysters in the shell*	2 T. chopped pimentos
Rock salt	¼ c. mayonnaise
2 T. chopped parsley	¼ tsp. salt
5 slices bacon, cut into 4 pieces each	¼ tsp. white pepper
	1 T. Worcestershire sauce
½ c. fine chopped bell pepper	1 lb. lump crab meat
1 tsp. dry mustard	1 c. soft bread crumbs
1 egg, beaten	¾ c. grated cheddar cheese

Scrub oysters well. Shuck the oysters and drain. This is how I shuck oysters and I think it will work best for you; place the blade of a large slotted screwdriver into the indented area behind the mussel and twist the handle, the oyster will pop open, next run a knife along the inside of the top shell and open. Save 20 of the oyster half shells. Cut each oyster into 3 or 4 pieces. Combine the oysters with the egg yolk, green pepper, pimentos, mustard, mayonnaise, salt, pepper, and Worcestershire sauce. Mix well. Gently fold in the crab meat. Place a bed of rock salt in a large baking pan to a depth of about ½ inch (you are probably going to need about 4 pounds of rock salt). Embed the 20 oyster shell halves into the rock salt and fill each one with the crab and oyster mixture, about 3 tablespoons. Top each with a sprinkling of bread crumbs and top this with a piece of bacon. Bake in a 350°, preheated, oven for 20 minutes. Remove from the oven, sprinkle with the cheese and parsley. Return to the oven for 5 more minutes. Serve as appetizers or main dish for 2. *Wash and save all the oyster shells, and the next time you want to make this dish or anything similar, you can use shucked oysters. Oyster shells can be used over and over again, just let them set in water for about 30 minutes before each use.

SHRIMP "N" GRITS

2¾ c. water	2 tsp. chopped, fresh parsley (opt.)
⅔ c. grits	
¼ tsp. salt	
½ lb. med. to lg. shrimp, peeled, deveined and chopped (save the shrimp shells)	

(continued)

27408F-99

Combine the shrimp shells and 1 cup of water in a 1-quart saucepan, bring to a boil, remove from heat and strain. Throw away the shells. Add the shrimp liquid back to the saucepan, add the remaining 1³/₄ cups of water. Bring to a boil and slowly stir in the salt and grits, reduce the heat to a simmer and 1 teaspoon parsley, cook for 3 minutes. Add the chopped shrimp and cook for another 4 minutes, stirring occasionally. Turn out into a bowl and garnish with 1 teaspoon parsley. Serve at breakfast or at dinner in place of mashed potatoes or rice. Serves 2 to 4.

BULL ISLAND BAKED SHRIMP

2 cloves garlic, crushed and
   minced real fine
¹/₄ c. olive oil
2 T. prepared Cajun seasoning
1 T. fresh lemon juice
1 T. fresh lime juice
2 T. fresh cilantro, chopped

1 T. honey
1 T. soy sauce
4 or 5 drops of Tabasco sauce
1 lb. raw shrimp, peeled and
   deveined (leave the tail section
   on)

Combine all of the ingredients listed above in a baking dish that measures about 9 x 13 inches and is at least 2 inches deep. Mix it up well so the shrimp gets coated well. Place the dish in the refrigerator and allow it to set at least 2 hours, or up until 4 hours, stir once about every hour. Preheat your oven to 450°. Place in the oven and bake for about 10 minutes; stir about 3 times during the baking. Serve with lemon wedges and a crusty French bread for sopping up the wonderful tasting juices.

BEER BATTER DEEP FRIED SHRIMP

2 lbs. med. or lg. shrimp, peeled
   and deveined, leaving tail
   section on
1¹/₂ c. self-rising flour

1¹/₂ c. beer
1 T. sugar
1¹/₂ c. all-purpose flour
4 c. peanut oil

Mix sugar, beer and self-rising flour and set aside. Coat shrimp with all-purpose flour and dip into batter mixture. Heat the oil in a 2-quart saucepan to 375°. Slowly drop shrimp, one at a time, into the hot oil. Cook until a golden brown (about one minute) and remove with a slotted

(continued)

27408F-99

spoon. Drain on clean dish towel, or paper towels. Serve with coleslaw and hush puppies. Serves 4 to 6.

SHRIMP AND OYSTER PARMESAN

½ c. grated Swiss cheese
⅛ c. grated Parmesan cheese
1 pt. half-and-half
1 tsp. fine chopped garlic
½ tsp. salt
½ tsp. white pepper
1 T. chopped cilantro

1 pt. oysters, drained
1 lb. med. shrimp, peeled and deveined
½ c. chardonnay wine
12 oz. linguine, cooked according to package directions

Heat a large heavy skillet over medium high heat, pour the wine in the skillet, add the shrimp and oysters to the skillet and cook until the edges curl up on the oysters and the shrimp just turns pink, about 1 minute, do not overcook. Remove the shrimp and oysters to a colander to drain and set aside. Drain the liquid from the skillet and discard. Reduce the heat to medium low, pour the half-and-half into the skillet and add the Swiss cheese, garlic, salt, pepper and cilantro. Cook until mixture starts to thicken, stirring constantly. Add the Parmesan cheese, drained linguine, shrimp and oysters, bring the heat back up to medium and cook just until mixture is hot. Serve immediately with a hot loaf of crusty, French bread. Serves 4 generously.

GOLDEN SHRIMP

12 extra lg. or jumbo shrimp, peeled and deveined
2 c. cooked penna pasta, keep warm
½ c. all-purpose flour
2 T. butter
1 T. capers

½ c. clear chicken broth
½ c. heavy cream
¼ c. chardonnay wine
½ c. canned coconut milk
1 sm. pinch saffron threads
1 T. oil
¼ c. grated Parmesan cheese

Lightly coat the shrimp with the flour and set aside. Over medium heat, heat a nonstick fry pan with the oil. Add the shrimp and cook to a light golden brown on each side (about 2 minutes on each side). Remove the shrimp and set aside. Pour the wine in the hot frying pan and cook for 1 minute. Add the chicken broth and coconut milk and reduce the liquid by half, add the heavy cream, butter, cappers and saffron; stir well to mix the ingredients. Simmer for 3 minutes stirring

(continued)

27408F-99

continuously. Add the shrimp and cook for 3 minutes, stirring occasionally; add the cooked pasta and Parmesan cheese and toss, serve immediately. Serves 2.

Note: I recommend a crust French or Cuban bread to accompany this dish.

SHRIMP ALEXANDRA

12 extra lg. or jumbo shrimp,
  peeled and deveined
2 c. cooked penna pasta, keep
  warm
½ c. all-purpose flour
2 T. butter
1 T. capers

½ c. clear chicken broth
½ c. heavy cream
¼ c. chardonnay wine
½ c. canned coconut milk
1 sm. pinch saffron threads
1 T. oil
¼ c. grated Parmesan cheese

Lightly coat the shrimp with the flour and set aside. Over medium heat, heat a nonstick fry pan with the oil. Add the shrimp and cook to a light golden brown on each side (about 2 minutes on each side). Remove the shrimp and set aside. Pour the wine in the hot frying pan and cook for one minute. Add the chicken broth and coconut milk and reduce the liquid by half, add the heavy cream, butter capers and saffron, stir well to mix the ingredients, simmer for 3 minutes stirring continuously. Add the shrimp and cook for 3 minutes stirring occasionally, add the cooked pasta and Parmesan cheese and toss, serve immediately. Serves 2.

Note: I recommend a crusty French or Cuban bread to accompany this dish.

COCONUT CURRY SHRIMP

1 (15-oz.) can chunk pineapple,
  drained
2 c. whole milk
3½ oz. flaked coconut
½ c. butter, melted and divided
  (make 2 little bowls)
⅓ c. chopped green onions

⅓ c. chopped celery
1 lb. med. fresh shrimp, peeled,
  leaving the tail section on
½ c. plain flour
¼ tsp. minced garlic
1 c. chicken broth
¼ c. Jamaican rum

Combine rum and coconut in a small saucepan and bring to a boil; add the milk and remove from the heat, let stand about 2 minutes.

(continued)

27408F-99

Strain the mixture placing the coconut in one bowl, and the coconut milk in another. Heat ¼ cup of the butter in a large skillet over medium heat (do not burn the butter), add the shrimp and pineapple chunks and sauté until the shrimp just turns pink, about 3 minutes or less (don't over cook). Drain the shrimp and set aside, throw away the liquid. Set the shrimp aside until I tell you to use them again. Combine the other ¼ cup of butter with the curry powder in that large skillet that you were just using and cook over low heat stirring constantly, do this for about 2 minutes. You are doing great, and you are going to love this dish. Next add the green onions and celery, continue cooking, stirring constantly until the vegetables are kind of crisp, but not burned, no more than 2 minutes. Remove the skillet from the heat and just let it rest there for a minute. Combine the garlic with the flour, and add it to the skillet, now stir and cook this mess for 1 minute, but stir the whole time it is cooking. Now, slowly add the coconut milk you saved and chicken broth (mix these two things together, it will make things easier) to the mixture you have in the skillet while cooking over medium heat, when this mixture becomes thickened and bubbly, stir in the coconut and shrimp, remove from the heat now and serve over rice. Should make 4 servings, and you will want to slap Chef Dirt for keeping this a secret for so long.

CHEF DIRT'S SHRIMP OMELET

(This is a must try for a quick and delicious meal)

6 oz. med. fresh shrimp, peeled and deveined	1 T. butter
2 sm. green onions, chopped fine	½ c. shredded mild cheddar cheese
1 T. butter	6 eggs
2 T. fresh milk	Home fries
2 tsp. chopped parsley	Hot biscuits
½ tsp. salt	Hollandaise sauce*
⅛ tsp. pepper	

Cut each shrimp in half, lengthwise down the vein. Sauté the shrimp and green onions in 1 tablespoon butter, just until the shrimp turn pink, about 1 minute. Remove from heat, add the parsley and mix. Combine the eggs, milk, salt and pepper, beat well. Heat a 10-inch skillet (non-stick will work best) over medium heat for 3 to 5 minutes, it should be real hot. Test by dropping 1 drop of water into the pan, if it sizzles it is hot enough. Add 1 tablespoon butter to the hot skillet and allow to melt, but not burn. Swirl the pan to coat the entire bottom with the butter. Add the egg mixture, as the eggs start to cook, lift the edges and allow

(continued)

27408F-99

the uncooked egg to run under the cooked part, do this until the eggs are just set (don't worry if a little bit in the center is not cooked). Remove the skillet from the heat and spoon the shrimp mixture over half the omelet, top with the cheese. Very gently loosen the un-filled side of the omelet with a spatula and fold over the filled side. Let stand for 2 minutes. Loosen the edges from the pan and gently slide to a warmed platter with home fried potatoes, top the omelet with the warm hollandaise sauce. This dish makes an elegant breakfast, lunch or dinner meal. Serve with Pepper Jelly and hot biscuits on the side. Serves 2 to 3.

*Note: If I have the time I will make my own hollandaise sauce, but due to the busy life style of most of us I recommend using the packaged mix kind, it will be good.

ASPIC SEAFOOD SALAD

2 env. unflavored gelatin
½ c. ice cold water
¼ c. ice cold water
3 c. clam juice
2 T. tomato paste
3 c. chopped celery, divided
¼ c. chopped green onion
1 T. Worcestershire sauce
Dash of salt
¼ tsp. white pepper

1 c. mayonnaise
1 c. whipping cream whipped
½ lb. med. shrimp, cooked, peeled and deveined
½ lb. sea scallops, steamed for 4 minutes
¾ lb. fresh tuna, cut into ½-inch cubes and steamed for 5 minutes

Sprinkle 1 envelope of gelatin over ½ cup of cold water and let stand for 1 minute. Combine the clam juice, 1 cup of celery, the green onion and the tomato paste in a saucepan and bring to a boil, cook for 1 minute. Remove from the heat and strain, discard the vegetables. Combine the vegetable liquid and gelatin mixture, stirring until the gelatin dissolves. Stir in the Worcestershire sauce, salt and pepper. Pour this mixture into a lightly oiled 11-cup mold. Chill until the consistency of unbeaten egg whites. Sprinkle 1 envelope of gelatin over ¼ cup of cold water in a saucepan and let stand for 1 minute. Cook over medium heat just until the gelatin dissolves. Remove from the heat and let cool. Fold the mayonnaise and the gelatin mixture into the whipped cream. Fold in the seafood and 2 cups of celery, gently spoon this mixture on top of the aspic mixture all ready in the mold. Refrigerate until firm, about 4 hours. Unmold onto a bed of lettuce and serve. Makes about 8 servings.

27408F-99

SHRIMP ALA SUGAR BRITCHES

2 lbs. lg. shrimp, peeled and
   deveined
1 tsp. dried dill weed
2 tsp. minced garlic
½ tsp. salt
1 tsp. lemon juice
1 T. white wine
1 c. butter

¼ tsp. thyme
1 tsp. coarse ground black pepper
¼ c. chopped green onions
1 T. chopped fresh parsley
3 lg. rolls, split and toasted (rolls
   should be sourdough or French)
1 c. melted butter

Combine the green onions, garlic and ¼ cup of the butter in a large skillet until the onions are tender. Add the shrimp, the remaining butter, lemon juice, wine, salt and pepper. Cook over medium heat for 4 minutes, stirring now and then. Add the parsley, dill weed and thyme. Stir to mix well. Spoon the mixture over the toasted roll halves, you only need to serve this with a salad and glass of your favorite wine. Makes 6 servings.

STEAMER POT FOR 4
(Outer Banks Style)

1 to 1½ lbs. smoked sausage, cut
   into 4 pieces
8 sm. new potatoes, cut in half
4 ears of corn, shucked
8 sm. pearl onions
24 little neck clams
8 hard crabs, cleaned outer banks
   style*

8 extra lg. shrimp, leave shell on
3 c. water
¼ c. Old Bay seasoning
¼ c. fresh parsley, chopped
1 c. melted butter (divide into four
   bowls for dipping)

Pour 3 cups of water into the bottom of a steamer pot (steamer pot should have a basket or tray to keep the ingredients off the bottom and out of the water), you will need about an 8-quart steamer pot. Layer potatoes, corn and smoked sausage in the bottom of the basket or on top of the tray, sprinkle with about ¼ of the Old Bay and about half the parsley, rotate corn to cover all around with Old Bay. Next, spread the clams over the potatoes and corn, sprinkle with Old Bay. Spread the crabs, cleaned side up over the clams and sprinkle generously with Old Bay (about 2 tablespoons). Lay shrimp and onions on top of crabs, sprinkle with remaining parsley. Cover pot and place over high heat until pot starts to steam (should take about 5 minutes) then reduce the heat to medium high and steam for 20 minutes. Dump the contents of the pot, but not the water, onto a very large platter or shallow pan.

(continued)

27408F-99

Serve immediately with hot butter on the side for dipping. Serves 4 generously. * To clean crabs outer banks style: the crabs must be alive and uncooked. Remove the top shell, pull out the dead man (or lungs). Remove the entrails from the center of the crab and rinse well.

Note: If hard crabs are not available, you may substitute with 4 snow crab clusters, only add them to the pot during the last 10 minutes of cooking time.

GILLED LOBSTER TAILS

4-6 oz. rock lobster tails, fresh (if frozen, make sure they are thawed)	¹⁄₂ c. mayonnaise
	¹⁄₄ tsp. fresh grated ginger
	2 cloves garlic, minced very fine
1 lemon	1 tsp. chili powder
2 T. olive oil	¹⁄₄ tsp. dried dill weed

Using a large sharp knife, cut through the top shell and the lobster meat, do not cut through the bottom shell. Spread the shell open, butterfly fashion and pull the meat to the top of the shell. Set the lobster aside. Grate the lemon to make ¹⁄₂ teaspoon of lemon zest (lemon peel) and set aside. Cut the lemon in half and squeeze out enough juice to make about 5 tablespoons. Mix half the lemon juice with the ginger, olive oil, garlic and chili powder. Brush the mixture on the exposed lobster meat and save the rest of the sauce. Heat the grill to a medium hot heat. Grill the lobster tails, meat side down for 7 to 10 minutes or until the meat turns opaque, turning once halfway through the cooking and basting with the saved sauce. Combine the mayonnaise, dill weed, remaining lemon juice in a bowl and mix well. Divide the dill sauce between 4 small bowls, and set one at each plate for dipping the lobster meat in. Serves 4.

Note: This is very important! Do not overcook the lobster meat!

CLAMS STEAMED IN WINE

¹⁄₂ c. carrots, sliced thin	1 tsp. salt
¹⁄₂ c. yellow onions, sliced thin	1 tsp. white pepper
¹⁄₂ c. celery, sliced thin	2 c. chardonnay wine
¹⁄₄ c. cilantro, chopped	4 doz. little neck or soft-shell
1 lemon, sliced thin	clams (also called piss-clams)

(continued)

27408F-99

Rinse clams with clean fresh water and set aside. (You may want to purge the clams to remove the sand. To do this, mix 2 quarts cold water with 1 tablespoon corn meal and let sit for 1 hour and drain.) In a large skillet, combine wine, carrots, onions, celery, cilantro, lemon slices, salt and pepper and bring to a boil. Add the clams to the boiling mixture; bring back to a boil, stirring the clams and mixture as it continues to cook. As soon as the clams start to open, remove them one at a time to a shallow bowl. When all of the clams have been removed to the shallow bowl, spoon about half of the vegetable and wine mixture over them and serve. Serves 4 as an appetizer.

DELICIOUS CLAM PIT

¼ lb. salt pork	3 sm. potatoes
1 sm. onion	20 sm. hard clams in juice
Water	2 T. butter, fat or oil
1 T. chopped parsley	1 c. cream
⅛ tsp. pepper	1 T. salt
¼ tsp. celery salt	3 T. flour

Dice the salt pork fine and let it fry out slowly in a frying pan. Then add the onion, minced fine and cook until it takes a golden brown color. Strain the clams and add to the clam juice enough water to make 3 cups of liquid. Add the liquid to the onions and the potatoes, diced, cook about 20 minutes or until the potatoes are tender. Then add the hard clams, cut into halves, the fat, the celery salt, salt, pepper and chopped parsley. Blend the flour with 2 tablespoons milk and add to the clam mixture while stirring. Last, add 1 cup of cream. Meanwhile prepare a rich pastry, using 1½ cups of pastry flour, ⅓ cup of shortening, ½ teaspoon of baking powder, ½ teaspoon of salt. Then gradually add enough cold water to make a soft dough, about 3 or 4 tablespoons of water will be required. Pour the clam mixture into a greased baking dish and cover with the pastry rolled to fit the baking dish. Bake at 500° for 15 minutes.

SUGAR BRITCHES FRIED LEGS

8 to 12 pairs of sm. frog legs, frog legs normally come frozen (unless you gig your own like Sugar Britches does) in pairs	2 T. fine ground black pepper
	1 tsp. ground thyme
	1 c. Seafood Breader (recipe is in this book)
½ tsp. salt	Corn or peanut oil

(continued)

27408F-99

Let the frog legs thaw in the refrigerator overnight. Mix together the salt, pepper and thyme, this is the pepper rub. Rub the frog legs with the pepper rub. Using a small basting brush, dampen the legs, but do not wash the rub off. Pour about 3 inches of oil in a 2-quart sauce pan and heat to 375°. Place the Seafood Breader in a plastic bag and add the frog leg pairs, 3 at a time, shake to coat, continue until you have them all coated with the breader, drop about 4 at a time into the hot oil and cook until golden brown, 2 to 3 minutes. Drain on paper towels and if you like serve with coleslaw, potato salad and hush puppies. Serves 2 to 4 depending on the size of the legs.

CRAB AND BEEF WELLINGTON

¾ c. butter
6 oz. creamed cheese, softened
1⅓ c. all-purpose flour
4 sm. filet mignon steaks, about ¾-inch thick
2 T. butter
¼ c. canned beef broth
¼ c. burgundy wine
1 lg. carrot, scraped and sliced thin
¾ c. sliced, fresh mushroom caps
½ c. shredded Swiss cheese
1 egg
1 tsp. water
8 oz. fresh lump crab meat, divided into 4 portions
Wellington sauce

Combine ¾ cup of butter and cream cheese in a medium-size mixing bowl and mix well. Add the flour and mix until moistened and forms a soft ball. Divide into four pieces, place on a buttered dish, cover with plastic wrap and refrigerate for 1 hour. Now to start the next part; melt 2 tablespoons butter in a medium-sized skillet over medium to medium high heat. Add the filet mignon steaks, sauté for 2 minutes on each side, remove and set aside to drain on paper towels. Pour the burgundy into the frying pan used to sauté the steaks and bring to a boil to deglaze the pan. Add the beef broth and carrots, reduce the heat to a simmer and cook for about 8 minutes, drain the carrots and set aside. Add 1 tablespoon butter to the skillet and sauté the mushrooms until tender, but still crisp (tender crisp), drain and set aside. Roll out each pastry portion on a floured surface until about ⅛ inch thick. Assemble the Wellington's as follows; place a filet mignon on top of a rolled out pastry, top with a portion of the crab meat, top this with ¼ of the carrots, mushrooms and cheese. Fold 2 opposite edges of the pastry over the filling; then fold over the 2 remaining edges to make an envelope. Place on an ungreased baking sheet, seam side down, repeat this with the other Wellington's. Combine the water and egg in a small mixing bowl and mix well, brush the tops and sides of each Wellington with the egg

(continued)

mixture. Bake in a preheated 425° oven for 15 minutes or until golden brown. Serve with Wellington Sauce.

Note: Do not wash the mushrooms, brush off with a clean, dry paper towel.

Wellington Sauce:

¾ **c. beef broth**
¾ **c. water**
3 **T. butter**
3 **T. all-purpose flour**

⅛ **tsp. salt**
¼ **tsp. pepper**
1 **T. capers, drained**

Combine broth and water and set aside. Melt the butter in a 1-quart saucepan, add the flour, salt and pepper. Cook over medium heat for about 1½ minutes, stirring constantly. Remove from the heat and add the broth/water mixture, and capers, stir to mix well. Return to medium heat and cook, stirring constantly, until thickened and reduced to about half. Spoon over Wellington.

MISSY'S OUTER BANKS CRAB IMPERIAL

4 **puff pastry shells (recipe in this book)**
2 **T. finely chopped shallots**
1 **T. finely chopped green peppers**
3 **T. butter**
1 **T. diced pimentos**
½ **tsp. dry mustard**
⅛ **tsp. dry whole thyme**

3 **T. all-purpose flour**
1 **c. milk**
1 **tsp. Worcestershire sauce**
¼ **tsp. salt**
1 **lb. lump crab meat**
3 **T. mayonnaise**
½ **c. grated cheddar cheese**

In a large skillet, sauté peppers and onions in butter, over medium low heat until tender, about 3 minutes. Remove from heat and stir in the pimentos, mustard and thyme. Add the flour and stir until blended, return to medium heat and cook until smooth, stirring continuously, about 3 or 4 minutes. Gradually add the milk while constantly stirring, keep stirring and cook until thick and bubbly, about 2 more minutes. Now stir in the Worcestershire sauce and pepper. Remove from the heat and fold in the mayonnaise and crab meat. Place mixture in a baking dish, cover with aluminum foil and bake in a 375° preheated oven for 15 minutes. Remove from oven and spoon the Imperial mixture into the 4 puff pastry cups. Place on a baking sheet, sprinkle the cheese over the top of the Imperials and place under the broiler for 1 minute, or until cheese is just melted, transfer the Imperials to individual serving

(continued)

27408F-99

plates and spread any remaining mixture over/around each Imperial. Serve immediately. Serves 4.

CRAB MEAT WITH PENNE PASTA AND BUTTER CREAM SAUCE

2 sticks butter (½ lb.)
2 T. all-purpose flour
1 lb. lump crab meat
2½ c. uncooked penne pasta
2 lg. cloves garlic, crushed and
  chopped real fine

1 T. chopped fresh cilantro
¼ tsp. salt
¼ tsp. white pepper
2 c. half-and-half
1 T. capers

Cook the pasta according to package directions, rinse with cold water and set aside. Melt about ½ stick of the butter in a 1-quart saucepan and add the flour, cook for about 2 minutes over medium heat or until creamy, stirring continuously. Add the salt, pepper, garlic and cilantro. Remove from the heat and slowly whisk in the half-and-half, return to a medium low heat and add the rest of the butter. Cook, whisking continuously until the butter is blended with the cream. Add the crab meat and fold gently into the sauce. Remove from the heat and set aside. Submerge the cooked pastas into boiling water and drain. Pour the pasta onto a large platter and cover with the crab/butter cream sauce. Serve with a fresh garden salad and a hot loaf of bread. Serves 4.

CRAB AND OYSTER CROQUETS

1 pt. oysters, drained
1 lb. backfin crab meat
¼ c. chopped celery
¼ c. chopped onion
1 T. Worcestershire sauce
1 T. Old Bay seasoning
14 slices white bread

2 T. chopped fresh parsley
¼ c. finely chopped fresh
  mushrooms
1 egg
1 T. butter
3 T. oil + 1 more, vegetable or
  corn

Combine the celery and onion in a skillet with the 1 tablespoon of oil and sauté the vegetables until tender, drain off the excess liquid and set aside. Add the oysters to the skillet you just used for the vegetables

(continued)

27408F-99

(make sure you have removed the vegetables first) and cook the oysters, over medium high heat for 1 minute.

Note: The 1 minute starts when the oysters actually start to cook, do not over cook them, you might think they are under cooked, but don't worry about it, they are just right. Set aside to cool. Once they have cooled for about 10 minutes, remove them from the cooking liquid and coarse chop them (each oyster should be in about 3 to 4 pieces). Now you need to make some bread crumbs. Using a food processor grind the white bread slices into fine crumbs, about 4 slices at a time. Set aside 3 cups of the bread crumbs and pour the rest into a large mixing bowl. Into the mixing bowl you just put the bread crumbs; dump in the oysters with their cooking liquid, the vegetables, the crab meat, the parsley, mushrooms and the Old Bay seasoning. Toss to blend. Using a small bowl, lightly beat the egg with the Worcestershire sauce and pour it into the crab/oyster mixture and mix everything well. Using about ½ cup of the mixture make some balls until you have used it all up. Roll each ball into the bread crumbs you saved and gently flatten them until they are about ½ inch thick, gently pat bread crumbs onto any wet areas, heat the 3 tablespoons oil and 1 tablespoon butter in a large non-stick fry pan over medium heat until golden brown, about 3 minutes on each side. Makes 12 to 15 croquets. If you have too many don't worry, you will have great sandwich makings for a couple of days. Serve with tartar sauce, mashed potatoes and a garden salad.

FLOUNDER, CRAB AND SHRIMP, ITS IN THE BAG!

½ lb. med. fresh shrimp, peeled
   and deveined
2 T. butter
3 T. butter
½ c. fresh, sliced mushrooms
   (never wash fresh mushrooms,
   brush them off with a dry paper
   towel)
½ c. chopped green onions
3 T. all-purpose flour
3 T. all-purpose flour (no this is
   not a repeat)
1 c. half & half milk

½ c. dry white wine
2 T. chopped red bell pepper
   (opt.)
⅛ tsp. each salt, pepper and
   paprika
Olive oil
4 flounder fillets
½ lb. fresh lump crab meat
2 c. milk, whole or skimmed will
   do
1 egg, beaten
Parchment paper (can usually be
   found next to the aluminum foil)

Flounders have 2 sides, the back is dark and the belly is white for presentation, you may want to use the white side, but it will not be as

(continued)

27408F-99

thick as the dark side. Wash the fillets with cold water and place in a bowl, add the 2 cups of milk and refrigerate for at least 30 minutes. Cut 8 pieces of parchment paper about 11 inches square. Melt 2 tablespoons of butter in a skillet, add the mushrooms and onions and sauté until tender. Melt 3 tablespoons of butter in a 1-quart or larger saucepan, over low heat. Add 3 tablespoons of flour and cook until smooth, about 1 to 2 minutes stirring constantly (or it will lump up on you). Gradually add the wine, then the half & half, stirring constantly, cook over medium heat until thickened and bubbly, stirring constantly. Stir in the mushroom mixture, salt, pepper and paprika, remove from heat and set this mixture aside. Place 4 sheets of the parchment paper on baking sheets, you may need to use 2 baking sheets. Lightly brush the top of the 4 sheets of paper with olive oil. Remove the fillets from the milk, rinse off with cold water and pat dry with paper towels. Place a fillet, skin side down, on each of the oiled paper sheets. Top each fillet with ¼ of the crab meat, shrimp and spoon the mushroom sauce over each, be careful and don't let the mushroom sauce run to the edges of the paper. Mix the beaten egg with 3 tablespoons of flour. This is the glue that will help hold the top and bottom sheets of parchment paper together. Brush the edges of the bottom sheet of paper with the glue mixture, place a top sheet of paper over the seafood and fold with the edges of the bottom sheet to make a sealed bag. Bake at 425° for 15 minutes, the bags will slightly brown and puff-up. Remove each bag to a serving plate using a spatula and being very careful. Just before serving, cut a slit in the top of each bag, be very careful, there is hot steam in there. Serve immediately with a garden salad and warm crusty bread. Makes 4 servings.

CRAB IMPERIAL IN PUFF PASTRY SHELLS

1 lb. fresh lump crab meat
1 recipe for Puff Pastry Shells
   (Recipe in this book)
¼ c. butter
½ c. grated mild cheddar cheese
2 T. all-purpose flour
1 c. milk

1 tsp. dry mustard
½ tsp. salt
⅛ tsp. white pepper
1 tsp. Worcestershire sauce
¼ c. soft bread crumbs
2 T. melted butter

Using a 1-quart or larger saucepan, melt ¼ cup of butter over low heat. Gradually add the flour stirring constantly. Cook until smooth (keep stirring) this will take about 1 minute. Gradually add the milk. Cook over medium heat, stirring constantly, until this mixture becomes thickened and bubbly, this will take about 3 minutes. Remove from the heat and add the mustard, salt, pepper and Worcestershire sauce, stir to mix

(continued)

well. Fold the crab meat into the sauce mixture, be extra careful not to break up the lumps. Pour the crab mixture into a medium-size casserole dish and bake in a 425° oven and bake for 10 minutes. Remove from the oven and fill the 4 puff pastry shells with the crab mixture. Sprinkle each with the bread crumbs and then the cheese. Place the filled pastry shells on a cookie sheet and bake in the same heated oven for 5 minutes. Place the Crab Imperials on individual plates and spoon any left over crab mixture around the pastry shells. Serve immediately.

RECIPE FAVORITES

27408F-99

SESAME

Breads
& Rolls

Helpful Hints

- Over-ripe bananas can be peeled and frozen in a plastic container until it's time to bake bread or cake.

- When baking bread, a small dish of water in the oven will help keep the crust from getting too hard or brown.

- Use shortening, not margarine or oil, to grease pans, as margarine and oil absorb more readily into the dough or batter (especially bread).

- Use a metal ice tray divider to cut biscuits in a hurry. Press into the dough, and biscuits will separate at dividing lines when baked.

- To make self-rising flour, mix 4 cups flour, 2 teaspoons salt and 2 tablespoons baking powder, and store in a tightly covered container.

- Hot water kills yeast. One way to tell the correct temperature is to pour the water over your forearm. If you cannot feel either hot or cold, the temperature is just right.

- When in doubt, always sift flour before measuring.

- When baking in a glass pan, reduce the oven temperature by 25°.

- When baking bread, you get a finer texture if you use milk. Water makes a coarser bread.

- If your biscuits are dry it could be from too much handling, or the oven temperature may not have been hot enough.

- Nut breads are better if stored 24 hours before serving.

- To make bread crumbs, toast the heels of bread and chop in a blender or food processor.

- Cracked eggs should only be used in dishes that are thoroughly cooked; they may contain bacteria.

- The freshness of eggs can be tested by placing them in a large bowl of cold water; if they float, do not use them.

- For a quick, low-fat crunchy topping for muffins, sprinkle the tops with Grape-Nuts cereal before baking.

Breads & Rolls

OLD TIME SHORTENING

½ c. lard   ½ c. butter

Soften and blend the lard with the butter, do not melt.

Note from the author: The early farm wife kept a small flock of ducks. On or the day before she did her baking, a duck (or ducks) would be slaughtered and baked. The fat would be reserved for the shortening she would be using in the baking of cookies, cakes, pies, etc. She would also use duck eggs in place of chicken eggs, because they were much richer.

SOUTHERN APPLE FRITTERS

1 egg, beaten well
¼ c. whole milk
2 tsp. granulated sugar
1 tsp. freshly ground cinnamon
1 sm. pinch freshly ground
   nutmeg
2 T. self-rising corn meal

1 c. self-rising flour
8 oz. sour cream
2 c. vegetable oil
3 Granny Smith apples, peeled,
   cored, sliced and diced into
   very fine pieces

Combine the first 7 ingredients, and mix well, add the sour cream and apples, stir to mix. Let stand for 5 minutes. Heat the oil to about 375° in a 2-quart saucepan. Your fritter batter should be about as thick as hushpuppie batter. You should be able, using 2 tablespoons (from your spoon drawer), form a sticky ball, if not add more flour until you can drop the fritters into the hot oil, by the rounded tablespoons, fry until golden brown. Remove from the hot oil with a slotted spoon and drain on paper towels. Dust with powdered sugar and serve hot. Makes about 10 to 15 fritters.

BUCKWHEAT PANCAKES

4 c. buckwheat flour
1 c. yellow Indian meal (yellow
   corn meal)
1 c. cold milk

3 c. hot water
1 yeast cake
1 tsp. soda
1 c. warm milk

(continued)

27408F-99

To 4 cups Buckwheat flour add 1 cup Indian meal and a tablespoon of salt. Mix one cup of milk with 3 cups hot water, and when the mixture is lukewarm beat it slowly into the dry ingredients to prevent lumping. Beat smooth, add one yeast cake dissolved in tepid water and continue beating five minutes. Put aside to rise about 7 o'clock in the evening in an earthen bucket with a tin cover. Before baking in the morning mix even teaspoon soda in a cup of warm milk and beat into the batter, which should form in bubbles. Pour the batter into a hot greased griddle in small, round cake. They should be a rich brown when baked (I think this means cook on top of the stove like you would pancakes). Serve with hot syrup and fresh butter. This should feed the whole family and the farm hands too.

SWEET MILK GRIDDLE CAKES

2 c. flour
1 T. baking powder
2 T. sugar
½ tsp. salt

1⅓ c. milk
1 egg, well beaten
2 T. melted butter

Sift together the dry ingredients; add the milk gradually, then the well-beaten egg and then the melted butter, beat thoroughly, pour on to a hot griddle or frying pan; flip once to cook on both sides.

CAROLINA WAFFLES

2 eggs, well beaten
1 pt. flour
1½ c. milk

A walnut size gob of butter
⅛ tsp. salt
1 tsp. baking powder

Mix the salt and baking powder well into the flour; rub the butter in evenly, then the well-beaten eggs and stir all into the milk. Have the waffle irons hot and well-greased, pour on the batter and bake quickly. The batter should be rather thin for good results.

27408F-99

SODA BISCUITS
(From 1877)

2 c. flour
¼ tsp. salt
½ tsp. baking soda

About 1 cup buttermilk
3 T. lard

Mix and sift dry ingredients and cut in lard. Add enough buttermilk to make soft dough. Knead lightly on a floured surface (4 or 5 times). Roll out to ¾ inch thick. Cut biscuits with floured biscuit cutter. Place biscuits on a greased cookie sheet and bake at 425°, 15 to 20 minutes. Makes 8 to 12 biscuits.

BAKING-POWDER BISCUITS

Before we get into making biscuits, I want to say a few words about it. Making a good biscuit is probably one of the hardest things in cooking to get right. I tell you right up front, it takes some practice. Luckily, biscuit making ingredients are cheap, so keep at it until you get it right, you eventually will get it right, and the rewards will be worth your persistence. Some people never get it right, mainly because they play around with them too long, or just get frustrated and quit. Don't you quit, I know you can do it. Now, here goes:

2 c. sifted flour, plain
3 tsp. baking powder
1 tsp. salt
6 tsp. lard

About ⅔ to ¾ c. buttermilk (you
    may use plain milk, but I don't
    think it is as good)

Start heating your oven to about 450°. Into a bowl, sift flour, baking powder, and salt, add the lard, and using a fork, cut in (by mashing) the lard until mixture is like corn meal. You are doing great! Now, dig out the center and make a well, pour in about ½ cup of milk. Now this is where you are going to have to get on the stick and don't fool around. With a fork, mix lightly and quickly. Add enough more milk to form dough that's just moist enough to leave the sides of the bowl and cling to the fork as a ball. Turn onto a floured surface for kneading. Knead this way; pick up side of dough farthest from you and with your palms press down, pushing dough away, be gentle. Turn the dough around and ¼ turn, now repeat this 6 more times, no more! Now, lightly roll the dough out from the center, using a floured rolling pen, if you don't have a rolling pen use a glass, a piece of an old broom handle about 10 inches long works best. Roll the dough to about ½ to ¾ inch thick for high fluffy biscuits or ¼ inch thick for thin crusty ones (these are my wife's

(continued)

favorite). You are doing great if you have mixed, kneaded, and rolled out the dough in less than 3 minutes. Now, cut the biscuits out using a 2-inch biscuit cutter (a tin can with both ends removed makes a great biscuit cutter). Dip biscuit cutter in flour before cutting each biscuit. Using a spatula, lift biscuits to an un-greased baking sheet and place just barely touching one another. Lightly press dough trimmings together; roll out and cut as before and place on the baking sheet. Lightly brush top of biscuits with bacon fat or butter, and bake for 12 to 15 minutes. Look at those great biscuits, aren't you proud of yourself. Makes about 16 biscuits.

MARYLAND MUFFINS

2 c. hot mashed potatoes	3 eggs
1 c. lard	¼ tsp. salt
½ c. warm water	2 T. sugar
1 cake yeast	Flour

Dissolve the cake of yeast in the warm water; add the lard, eggs and mashed potatoes. Mix well. Let stand in a warm place until light, about 1½ hours. Add 2 tablespoons sugar, salt and enough flour to make a soft dough. Let stand again to get light, after light. Make into biscuits and bake in a moderate oven, in greased pans.

BECKY'S CORN MUFFINS
(These muffins are extra light and sweet)

1 c. self-rising flour	2 T. corn or vegetable oil
¼ c. self-rising corn meal	½ c., less 2 T., milk
¼ tsp. salt	3 eggs, separated
1 T. sugar	

Place a medium-size bowl in the refrigerator to chill about 15 minutes. Lightly grease and dust with flour, a 12-cup muffin pan. Preheat the oven to 425°. Combine the flour, corn meal, salt and sugar in a bowl and mix well. Scoop out a well in the center and drop in 2 of the egg yolks (throw the third one away, or save for another dish). And the oil, set aside. Remove the chilled bowl from the refrigerator and pour in the egg whites. Using an electric mixer or wire whip beat the egg whites until you can form peaks. Place beaten egg whites in the refrigerator until you are ready to use them. Add the milk, all at once, to the flour

(continued)

27408F-99

mixture and mix just until the lumps are gone, no more. Very gently, fold in the beaten egg whites. Spoon the batter into each muffin pan cup to about ¾ full. Bake immediately for 13 minutes. Remove from the oven and remove the muffins from the pan. Serve warm, with soft butter. Makes 12 muffins.

GRIDDLE CAKES

1 c. whole-wheat flour
1 c. plain flour
3 tsp. baking powder
½ tsp. salt
2 T. sugar

1½ c. milk
1 egg
2 T. melted lard (you may
　　substitute corn oil)

Mix whole-wheat flour, plain flour, baking powder, salt and sugar together. Add milk, beaten egg and melted lard; mix well. Drop by tablespoons on hot, well-greased griddle and cook until golden brown on each side. Makes about 20 cakes.

CHEF DIRT'S' CITY BISCUITS

1 pkg. dry yeast
3 T. warm water
1 c. buttermilk, that has been
　　sitting out at room temperature
　　for 1 hour
2½ c. all-purpose flour

3 T. sugar
2 tsp. baking powder
½ tsp. baking soda
¾ tsp. salt
½ c. shortening

Combine the yeast and water, let stand for 5 minutes, add the buttermilk and set aside. In a large bowl, mix together the flour, sugar, baking powder, soda and salt, mix well to combine all ingredients. Add the shortening to the flour mixture, using a fork, cut in the shortening until the flour mixture resembles corn meal. Add the buttermilk and with a fork, mix until moistened. Turn the combined mixture out onto a floured surface and knead about 5 times. Roll the kneaded dough out until about ½ inch thick. Cut with a 2½ to 3-inch biscuit cutter (I collect an assortment of tin cans and remove both ends, these make excellent biscuit and cookie cutters). Place the cutout biscuits on a lightly greased cookie sheet, cover and let rise for 1 hour, and bake in a preheated oven at 450° for 10 to 12 minutes. Makes about 10 biscuits. Serve with honey butter.

27408F-99

SOUTHERN CRACKLING BREAD

1½ c. cornmeal
½ c. all-purpose flour
½ tsp. baking soda
½ tsp. salt
1 c. milk
2 eggs, beaten

2 T. bacon drippings (you may
   substitute for corn oil)
1½ c. shredded cheddar cheese
1 (8-oz.) can cream-style corn
¼ c. chopped green onions
2 c. cracklings

Cracklings are pieces of cooked pork fat, that are obtained as a result of rendering raw pork fat to make lard, they can be purchased in the meat section of most grocery stores.

1 T. oil

Start heating oven to 350° with a 10-inch cast iron frying pan inside. Combine the cornmeal, flour, soda and salt in a medium-size bowl and mix well. Add the milk, egg and bacon drippings. Stir just enough to moisten. Add all the remaining ingredients and mix until all ingredients are combined. Remove the 10-inch frying pan from the oven, (be very careful, the pan is very hot), add the 1 tablespoon of oil to the hot frying pan and swirl to coat the pan. Add the cornmeal mixture and place the frying pan back into the hot oven. Bake for about 30 minutes or until golden brown. Cut into wedges and remove from the pan as soon as possible. Makes 8 wedges. Serve with fresh creamery butter.

RECIPE FAVORITES

27408F-99

NUTMEG

Pies, Pastry & Desserts

Helpful Hints

- Egg whites need to be at room temperature for greater volume when whipped. Remember this when making meringue.

- When preparing several batches of pie dough, roll dough out between sheets of plastic wrap. Stack the discs in a pizza box, and keep the box in the freezer. Next time you're making pie, pull out the required crusts.

- Place your pie plate on a cake stand when placing the pie dough in it and fluting the edges. The cake stand will make it easier to turn the pie plate, and you won't have to stoop over.

- Many kitchen utensils can be used to make decorative pie edges. For a scalloped edge, use a spoon. Crosshatched and herringbone patterns are achieved with a fork. For a sharply pointed effect, use a can opener to cut out points around the rim.

- Dipping strawberries in chocolate? Stick toothpicks into the stem end of the berry. Coat the berries with chocolate, shaking off any excess. Turn the berries upside down and stick the toothpick into a block of styrofoam until the chocolate is set. The finished berries will have chocolate with no flat spots. Another easy solution is to place dipped berries dipped-side up in the holes of an egg carton.

- Keep strawberries fresh for up to ten days by refrigerating them (unwashed) in an airtight container between layers of paper towels.

- When grating citrus peel, bits of peel are often stuck in the holes of the grater. Rather than waste the peel, you can easily brush it off by using a clean toothbrush.

- To core a pear, slice the pear in half lengthwise. Use a melon baller to cut out the central core, using a circular motion. Draw the melon baller to the top of the pear, removing the interior stem as you go.

- When cutting up dried fruit, it sometimes sticks to the blade of the knife. To prevent this problem, coat the blade of your knife with a thin film of vegetable spray before cutting.

- Cutting dessert bars is easier if you score the bars as soon as the pan comes out of the oven. When the bars cool, cut along the scored lines.

- When cutting butter into flour for pastry dough, the process is made easier if you cut the butter into small pieces before adding it to the flour.

Pies, Pastry & Desserts

DIRT'S' CHESS PIE

¼ c. butter, melted but not hot
1 (9-inch) raw pastry shell
⅛ tsp. fresh ground nutmeg
1 T. plain cornmeal
1 T. all-purpose flour
4 eggs, beaten

¼ c. milk
1 T. lemon zest (this is the peel of the lemon, make sure the white skin is not included)
¼ c. lemon juice
1½ c. sugar

Combine the eggs, lemon juice, lemon zest and milk in a bowl and mix well. Combine the flour, sugar and cornmeal in another bowl and mix lightly. Slowly add the flour and cornmeal mixture to the egg mixture while stirring. Mix until smooth; stir in the butter. Now pour the pie filling mixture into the pie shell. Sprinkle the nutmeg over the top of the pie. Bake in a preheated 350° oven for about 45 minutes or until the filling is set. Cool on a wire rack for about 1 hour. Makes 1 (9-inch) pie.

COCONUT CUSTARD PIE

4 eggs, slightly beaten
½ c. white sugar
½ tsp. salt
1 tsp. vanilla
2 c. milk
½ tsp. fresh ground nutmeg

½ c. & ¼ c. grated coconut (for a plain custard pie, leave out the coconut)
1 baked (9-inch) pie shell (do not bake the shell until edges are brown)

Preheat the oven to 350°. Combine eggs, sugar, salt, vanilla, milk, ½ cup coconut and beat well. Pour the egg mixture into the baked pie shell. Sprinkle with nutmeg and ¼ cup of coconut. Place in the center of the oven and bake for 35 minutes or until silver knife inserted in the center comes out clean. Place pie on a wire pie rack and let cool for 20 minutes before serving.

DELLA'S VANILLA ICE CREAM

1½ c. milk
¾ c. sugar
2 T. flour
A few grains salt

2 eggs
1½ tsp. vanilla extract
1½ c. heavy cream

(continued)

73

If you have one of those new electric ice cream makers you can use it for this recipe. I want one but Roy said "We had enough electric things to eat up juice already, and the crank machine will do just fine." In a double boiler, scald the milk, mix the sugar, flour and salt. Stir in enough milk to make a smooth paste. Stir the rest of milk in the double boiler. Stir until thickened and cook, covered, for 10 minutes. Beat eggs slightly and stir in milk mixture. Return to the double boiler and cook for 1 minute. Cool and add the vanilla and cream. Pour mixture into the ice cream machine bucket, pack ice and salt around the bucket and turn the crank until it gets hard to turn. I like to serve this with my chocolate sauce and if you like you could add fresh fruit or berries to the cream before you freeze it.

PUFF PASTRY SHELLS

**1 recipe for Puff Pastry (recipe in
this book)**

Preheat oven to 425°. Unfold pastry and roll out again if necessary to make perfectly flat and even (pastry should be about ⅛ inch or less thick). Cut 8 (3-inch rounds) from the rolled out pastry, cover with a wet dish towel. Dampen the inside of 4 large muffin cups, or a muffin pan, with cold water. Gently press 2 pastry rounds, one at a time into each of the 4 muffin cups, you will probably end up with some uneven tops and fluted edges, this is alright, do not attempt to trim them. Place the muffin pan in the freezer for 10 minutes. Remove the muffin pan from the freezer and go directly to the heated oven. Bake until puffed and golden. Remove the pastry cups from the pan and allow to cool on a wire rack. Fill the cups with fruit, creamed vegetables, Crab Imperial, or what ever you like.

PUFF PASTRY

¼ **c. butter, chilled**
1¾ **c. all-purpose flour, chilled**
½ **c. ice cold water**
¼ **c. all-purpose flour, chilled**
¾ **c. butter, softened**

Using a pastry blender or a fork, cut ¼ cup of butter into 1¾ cups of flour, mixture should resemble coarse cornmeal. Sprinkle ½ cup of ice cold water over the flour and butter mixture. Stir with a fork until the dry ingredients are moistened. Shape into a ball, cover with plastic wrap or wax paper and refrigerate for 20 minutes. Combine the ¾ cup of

(continued)

27408F-99

softened butter and the ¼ cup of flour, stir this mixture until smooth, it is best to use a wooden spoon. Shape into a 6-inch square on waxed paper and refrigerate for 5 to 8 minutes. Roll the dough into a circle about 15 inches on a lightly floured surface (if you have or can find a pastry cloth, this will work best for rolling). Place the butter mixture in the center of the dough. Fold the left side of dough over the butter, next, fold the right side of the dough over the left. Now fold the upper and lower edges of the dough over the butter, making a thick square. Now this next step you will have to work real quick; place the dough, folded side down on a lightly floured surface or pastry cloth and roll into a 20 x 8-inch rectangle. Fold the rectangle into thirds to resemble a folded letter (begin the fold from the short side), Repeat the toll and fold procedure one more time. Wrap the dough in wax paper and refrigerate for about 2 hours. Repeat rolling, folding, and chilling procedure for 2 more times, then chill for at least 3 hours or overnight before using. Use this pastry to make pastry cups, apple or fruit dumplings, pie shells or whatever you like. Makes one recipe of Puff Pastry.

9-INCH PIE CRUST

⅓ c. + 1 T. lard   ½ tsp. salt
1 c. flour   2 to 3 T. cold water

If the pie calls for a 2 crust pie, double the recipe and divide in half. Cut the lard into the flour and salt until the particles are the size of small peas. Sprinkle in the water, one tablespoon at a time, tossing with a fork until all the flour has been moistened and pastry wants to cling to the side of the bowl. If pastry seems to be too dry, add melted lard (not hot) to the mixture, by the teaspoonful. Roll pastry into a ball and turn onto a floured surface. Using a floured rolling pin or piece of broom handle, roll out to fit a 9-inch pie pan (about 14-inches in diameter).

RECIPE FAVORITES

Recipe Favorites

MINT

Cakes, Cookies
& Candy

Helpful Hints

- Push animal shaped cookie cutters lightly into icing on cakes or cupcakes. Fill depressed outlines with chocolate icing or decorating confections.

- Fill flat bottomed ice cream cones half full with cake batter and bake. Top with icing and decorating confections.

- Marshmallows can be used for candle holders on cakes.

- To keep the cake plate clean while frosting, slide 6-inch strips of waxed paper under each side of the cake. Once the cake is frosted and the frosting is set, pull the strips away leaving a clean plate.

- When decorating a cake with chocolate, you can make a quick decorating tube. Put chocolate in a heat-safe zipper-lock plastic bag. Immerse in simmering water until the chocolate is melted. Snip off the tip of one corner, and you can squeeze the chocolate out of the bag.

- Professionally decorated cakes have a silky, molten look. To get that appearance, frost your cake as usual, then use a hair dryer to blow-dry the surface. The slight melting of the frosting will give it that lustrous appearance.

- To ensure that you have equal amounts of batter in each pan when making a layered cake, use a kitchen scale to measure the weight.

- To make cookie crumbs for your recipes, put cookies into a plastic bag and run a rolling pin back and forth until they are the right size.

- To decorate cookies with chocolate, place cookies on a rack over waxed paper. Dip the tines of a fork with chocolate, and wave the fork gently back and forth making wavy lines.

- A gadget that works well for decorating sugar cookies is an empty plastic thread spool. Simply press the spool into the dough, imprinting a pretty flower design.

- Some holiday cookies require an indent on top to fill with jam or chocolate. Use the rounded end of a honey dipper to make the indent.

- When a recipe calls for packed brown sugar, fill the correct size measuring cup with the sugar, and then use the next smaller size cup to pack the brown sugar into its cup.

Cakes, Cookies & Candy

RICH FRUIT CAKE

(First printed in the "North American" newspaper in 1918.)

Note: All spoon measurements are rounding unless otherwise stated.

1 c. butter	½ c. orange or lemon peel
2 c. sugar	½ c. blanched Jordan almonds,
6 eggs	sliced thin or chopped pecans
½ c. milk or grape juice	½ c. thinly sliced figs
1 c. seeded raisins	3½ c. flour
½ c. chopped seeded raisins	2 tsp. baking powder
1 c. whole seedless raisins	½ tsp. grated nutmeg
½ c. thinly sliced citron	1 tsp. ground cinnamon

Cream the butter and sugar until light; add the well beaten yolks of eggs and milk slowly; beat until light and then add the fruit, which you sprinkle with ½ cup of flour; mix well; sift the 3 cups of flour with baking powder, add half the flour, then add the well beaten whites of eggs, the rest of the flour. Line the pan or pans with 3 thickness of paper (I think they mean parchment paper); place in moderate oven and bake 1½ to 2 hours. As soon as cake is cool, wrap in waxed paper and put in box.

Note from the author: I think it is intended to let this cake age for about 2 weeks and the box is a cake tin much like we get with modern day, premium fruit cakes.

RHUBARB AND STRAWBERRY PIE

Pastry for a 2 crust (9-inch) pie	4 c. rhubarb, cut into 11½-inch
1½ c. sugar	pieces
⅓ c. + 1 T. flour	½ tsp. grated orange peel
2 c. washed and quartered	2 T. butter
strawberries	

Combine sugar, flour and orange peel and set aside. Preheat oven to 425°. Prepare pastry. Lightly grease a 9-inch pie pan. Put 1 table-spoon flour in the greased pie pan and shake it around the pan until a light coating of flour has coated the greased pie pan, and dump out all the loose flour. Press half the pastry dough into the greased and floured pie pan. Turn half of the rhubarb into the pastry lined pie pan. Cover with half the sugar mixture. Cover with the strawberries. Cover with the remaining rhubarb, cover with remaining sugar mixture and dot with

(continued)

butter. Cover with the top crust, and pinch edges all around pie to seal the bottom crust with the top. Cut about 4 or 5 slits in the top crust about 2 inches (to allow steam to escape while baking). Bake 40 to 50 minutes or until crust is browned and juices begins to boil out of slits in top of crust. If you have never had strawberry/rhubarb pie, you don't know what you have been missing!!!

BLACK CHOCOLATE CAKE

2 oz. chocolate (unsweetened)	¼ tsp. salt
½ c. boiling water	1 c. flour
4 T. shortening (see recipe for shortening)	¾ tsp. soda
	4 T. sour milk
1 c. sugar	1 egg

Melt the chocolate and shortening with water, beating slightly until glossy. After removing from fire, add the sugar, salt, flour and soda sifted together, then the sour milk. Beat hard for a minute and add the egg. Beat 2 minutes more and pour into greased layer cake pans. Bake in a moderate oven about 20 minutes. Prepare the following filling.

Orange filling:

6 T. butter	1 c. orange juice
1 c. sugar	1 egg white, beaten stiff
Yolks of 3 eggs, well beaten	3 tsp. grated orange rind

Melt the sugar and butter together, then add the orange juice, rind and egg yolks, beating constantly. Cook about 8 minutes, continuing the stirring and fold in the egg white thoroughly. Put between the layers of cake and place cake on wooden plank or board covered with brown paper. Cover cake with a meringue made of five egg whites, beaten stiff, ¼ teaspoon of cream of tartar, ¼ cup of sugar and 1 teaspoon flavoring (like vanilla). Sprinkle the top and sides with granulated sugar, then brown quickly in a hot oven (about 5 minutes). Remove from board and paper onto platter and serve.

PECAN PRALINE CANDY

2 c. white sugar	2 T. butter
1 tsp. baking soda	2⅓ c. pecan halves
1 c. buttermilk	⅔ c. perfect pecan halves
⅛ tsp. salt	

(continued)

27408F-99

In a large kettle, about an 8-quart size, combine the sugar, buttermilk and salt. Cook over high heat about 5 minutes or until the mixture reaches 210° on a candy thermometer, while you are doing this be very sure to stir often and scrape the bottom and the sides of the kettle. Add the butter, 2⅓ cups of pecans, and cook for 5 minutes or until mixture forms a soft ball when a small amount is dropped in water (230° on a candy thermometer), make sure you stir and scrape, sides and bottom of the kettle while cooking. Cool the candy slightly, about 1 or 2 minutes, then with a spoon, beat until thickened and creamy. Immediately drop by tablespoonfuls onto a lightly buttered surface or waxed paper. Top each praline with the perfect pecan halves, pressing down gently to imbed the pecan halves into the praline. Makes 6 to 8 pralines.

PEANUT BRITTLE

2 c. granulated sugar
1 c. packed brown sugar
½ c. white corn syrup
½ c. water
⅛ tsp. baking soda

⅛ tsp. salt
¼ c. butter
1¼ c. parched peanuts (do not oil
   or salt the parched peanuts)

In a medium-size saucepan, combine the corn syrup, both sugars, and water. Bring the mixture to a slow boil while stirring continuously. Continue cooking after it comes to a slow boil, but do not stir any more. Now you have to watch it very closely, when a little bit of the mixture dropped in water becomes very brittle immediately remove it from the heat (or when it reaches 300° on a candy thermometer). Add the soda, salt and butter, stir only enough to mix add the peanuts and stir 2 or 3 times, do this quickly and avoid scraping the bottom of the pan. Pour the mixture, all at once onto a lightly buttered 12 x 18-inch cookie sheet, don't scrape the bottom of the pan, leavings will be sugary. Allow cooling about 1 minute, then take hold of candy at edges and lying out onto a lightly buttered surface, such as a counter top and pulling quite thin. When the candy is cold, break it up and store in an airtight container.

MOLASSES CANDY
(Pulled Taffy)

4 c. sugar
2 c. molasses

½ c. vinegar
1 T. baking soda

(continued)

79

Combine all ingredients in a large pot and boil until it crisps in cold water (I think what is meant here is "cook the mixture until it forms a hard ball when a drop of it is placed in a glass of water"). Stir in 1 tablespoon baking soda. Pour into small buttered dishes and when sufficiently cool pull it until it is light and elastic, this works best with two people with lightly buttered hands. Cut into small pieces and individually wrap with wax paper.

PECAN FUDGE

This is a recipe from my "Down Memory Lane" cookbook, it belonged to my mother. I have been making it since my early teen years and it is my favorite fudge recipe, that is why I have included it in this book, I think it will become your favorite also.

2 c. white sugar	**2 T. white corn syrup**
1 c. milk	**2 T. butter**
½ tsp. salt	**½ tsp. vanilla extract**
2 sq. unsweetened chocolate	**½ c. coarse chopped pecans**

Combine the sugar, milk, salt, chocolate and corn syrup in a 2-quart saucepan and cook over low heat until the sugar dissolves. Continue cooking gently, stirring occasionally until the temperature on a candy thermometer reaches 238°, or until a drop of the mixture dropped into a glass of cold water forms a soft ball (this step is the most important one in the making of the candy, so watch it very close, if you overcook it, it will be gritty). Once you have got this far, remove the pan from the heat quickly. Add the butter, don't you dare stir it! Let the mixture cool until it is about 110°, or until the pan just feels warm to the touch. Add the vanilla. If you have one of the new electric mixers, this next step will be easy, if not your hand and arm is going to get awfully tired. Beat the candy until it loses its glossy look. Add the pecans and from here move real fast. Just stir enough to get the pecans mixed in, turn the candy out onto a lightly buttered platter and spread out as best you can. Allow to set until completely cool and cut into squares.

SOUTHERN PRALINES

2 c. granulated sugar	**2 T. butter**
1 tsp. baking soda	**2⅓ c. pecan halves**
1 c. buttermilk	**⅔ c. perfect pecan halves**
⅛ tsp. salt	

(continued)

27408F-99

In a large kettle, about an 8-quart size, combine the sugar, buttermilk and salt. Cook over high heat about 5 minutes or until the mixture reaches 210° on a candy thermometer, while you are doing this be very sure to stir often and scrape the bottom and the sides of the kettle. Add the butter, 2⅓ cups of pecans, and cook for 5 minutes or until mixture forms a soft ball when a small amount is dropped in water (230° on a candy thermometer), make sure you stir and scrape, sides and bottom of the kettle while cooking. Cool the candy slightly, about 1 or 2 minutes, then with a spoon, beat until thickened and creamy. Immediately drop by tablespoonfuls onto a lightly buttered surface or waxed paper. Top each praline with the perfect pecan halves, pressing down gently to imbed the pecan halves into praline. Makes 6 to 8 pralines.

DIVINITY CANDY

2⅓ c. white sugar
⅔ c. white corn syrup
½ c. water
¼ tsp. salt
2 egg whites

½ c. walnuts
½ tsp. almond extract (you may use vanilla if you want)
2 T. shredded coconut

Combine in a 2-quart saucepan; sugar, corn syrup, water and salt. Stir over low heat until the sugar dissolves. Cover and boil for 1 minute, or until all sugar crystals on the side of the pan have melted. Uncover and cook gently, without stirring, to 265° on a candy thermometer, or until a little mixture in cold water forms a ball that is almost brittle. Beat the egg whites until stiff and forms peaks, an electric mixer on high speed will make quick work of this or you may do it by hand with a wire whip. Slowly pour the syrup into the beaten egg whites, beating until mixture looses its gloss and small amount dropped from the spoon holds its shape. Add the nuts, coconut, and vanilla and very gently fold into the mixture. Drop by teaspoonful onto a lightly buttered pan. Do not scrape the pan. Sprinkle with grated chocolate. (Place chocolate in the freezer for about 15 minutes, this will make it much easier to grate).

PLAIN CAKE WITH MOCHA ICING

⅓ c. shortening
1 c. sugar
½ c. milk

2 egg yolks
1½ c. flour
2 level tsp. baking powder

(continued)

Mix sugar and shortening until creamy. Add yolks of egg and milk slowly; add sifted flour and baking powder. Mix lightly; bake in 2 jelly tins that have been brushed with butter and dusted with flour, for 20 minutes.

Icing:

½ c. confectioners' sugar   1 rounded tsp. melted butter
Strong hot coffee

Mix the confectioners' sugar with a very little strong hot coffee and 1 teaspoon of melted butter until smooth and thick. Spread between and over top of cake. This will dry in an hour.

APPLESAUCE SPICE CAKE

½ c. shortening*   2½ tsp. baking powder
¾ c. sugar   1 tsp. salt
¾ c. molasses   1½ T. ginger
2 eggs   2 c. flour
½ c. milk

Applesauce filling:

2 c. applesauce   ½ tsp. cinnamon
¼ tsp. cloves   ½ tsp. nutmeg

Combine the applesauce, cloves, cinnamon and nutmeg and set aside. Combine and cream the shortening, sugar, molasses and eggs. Add the milk, baking powder, salt, ginger and flour, mix just until mixture is moist dough. Turn dough out on a floured surface and knead as you would for biscuits. Divide dough into 8 pieces and roll each piece into a ball. Preheat oven to 400°. Place one dough ball into a greased, round, cake pan and mash down to cover the bottom of the pan. Bake until just golden brown, about 10 minutes. Allow cooling slightly and removing from the pan. Cake layer will be about the size of a large pancake, repeat the process with the other 7 dough balls. Bake no more than 2 layers at a time. **Cake Assembly:** Place one cake layer on a plate and spread about ¼ cup of the applesauce filling over the layer, cover with another cake layer and filling. Continue this process until all eight layers have been stacked. Do not put applesauce mixture on top of the last layer. *Shortening in early kitchens was rendered fat from a baked duck, you may use creamed shortening such as Crisco.

27408F-99

PLANTATION DATE NUT BREAD

2 c. chopped dates
1 c. coarse chopped pecans
½ c. raisins
2 tsp. baking soda
2 c. hot water
1½ c. sugar

2 eggs, separated
3 c. flour
3 tsp. baking powder
¼ tsp. salt
6 to 8 tin cans, about the size of
    baking powder cans

Mix dates, raisins, and baking soda in a small pan, cover with hot water. Cook for 5 minutes and cool. Grease the inside of the tin cans. Beat egg whites stiff and set aside. Cream the sugar and egg yolks and add to the dates. Add the flour and baking powder, then the egg whites. Fill the tin cans ⅔ full. Cook on a cookie sheet in a 350° oven for about 30 minutes or until cake tester inserted into the center of one of the cakes comes out dry. Remove from the oven and immediately wrap the sides on each can with wet towels. Let stand for about 10 minutes and remove from the cans.

COMPANY CREAM CAKE

2 hen eggs
1 c. thick cream
½ tsp. salt
1 c. sugar

1 tsp. vanilla
3 tsp. baking powder
2 c. flour

Beat eggs in a bowl with the vanilla, gradually adding sugar while beating. Mix in flour, salt, cream and baking powder. Beat 25 to 30 strokes, do not overbeat. Pour batter into a greased and floured 9 x 13-inch baking pan. Bake at 350° for 30 minutes or until a broom straw inserted in the middle comes out dry. Allow to cool (about an hour), and cover with vanilla flavored, sweetened whipped cream. Cut and serve.

POUND CAKE WITH STRAWBERRY BRANDY TOPPING

6 eggs
1½ c. butter
3 c. sugar
1½ tsp. vanilla extract
1½ tsp. lemon extract

4½ c. flour
1 tsp. salt
¾ tsp. baking soda
¾ tsp. baking powder
1½ c. buttermilk

(continued)

27408F-99

Cream butter, gradually adding sugar, beat until light and fluffy. Add eggs and beat for 2 or 3 minutes. Blend in vanilla and lemon extract. Mix in all other ingredients, mixing only until well blended (do not over mix). Pour batter into 2 greased loaf pans. Bake at 350° for about 1 hour and 20 minutes or until broom straw inserted in the middle comes out dry. Cool in pans on wire rack for about 10 minutes. Remove from pans an slice and serve after completely cool. Can be served with ice cream or Strawberry Brandy Topping.

Note: Also good with chocolate gravy.

Strawberry Brandy Topping:

2 qt. wild or garden strawberries
½ c. sugar
3 T. brandy (you may leave out if
you don't have any or add rum, if
you like)

Chop strawberries and put in a bowl, add sugar and brandy, cover and let stand for 4 hours. Ladle generously over pound cake or use as topping for ice cream.

Recipe Favorites

27408F-99

DILL

This
& That

Helpful Hints

- To refinish antiques or revitalize wood, use equal parts of linseed oil, white vinegar and turpentine. Rub into the furniture or wood with a soft cloth and lots of elbow grease.

- To stop the ants in your pantry, seal off cracks where they are entering with putty or petroleum jelly. Also, try sprinkling red pepper on floors and counter tops.

- To fix sticking sliding doors, windows and drawers, rub wax along their tracks.

- To make a simple polish for copper bottom cookware, mix equal parts of flour and salt with vinegar to create a paste. Store the paste in the refrigerator.

- Applying baking soda on a damp sponge will remove starch deposits from an iron. Make sure the iron is cold and unplugged.

- Remove stale odors in the wash by adding baking soda.

- To clean Teflon™, combine 1 cup water, 2 tablespoons baking soda and ½ cup liquid bleach. Boil in stained pan for 5 to 10 minutes or until the stain disappears. Wash, rinse, dry and condition with oil before using the pan again.

- Corning Ware can be cleaned by filling it with water and dropping in two denture cleaning tablets. Let stand for 30 to 45 minutes.

- A little instant coffee will work wonders on your wood furniture. Just make a thick paste from instant coffee and a little water, and rub it into the nicks and scratches on your dark wood furniture. You'll be amazed at how new and beautiful those pieces will look.

- For a clogged shower head, boil it for 15 minutes in a mixture of ½ cup vinegar and 1 quart water.

- For a spicy aroma, toss dried orange or lemon rinds into the fireplace.

- Tin coffee cans make excellent freezer containers for cookies.

- Add raw rice to the salt shaker to keep the salt free-flowing.

- Ice cubes will help sharpen garbage disposal blades.

This & That

HOW TO DRESS BIRDS

First you will need to dry pick, to do this hang the bird up by one leg. Pluck the pinion and tail feathers first, then the small feathers from the shanks and inside of thighs, then pluck the remaining body feathers. Grasp only a few of the feathers and pull down in the direction the feather grows, this will avoid tearing of the skin, which you want to avoid. Using a sharp knife, slit the belly skin from the rib cage to the tail (much the same as you would a chicken), remove the entrails, save the giblets (liver, gizzard, and heart). Wash the inside of the bird using clean, fresh water, refrigerate until ready to cook. Birds that eat fish will sometimes have a fishy taste. Some people don't like this, if you are one, you may remove this by parboiling the bird for about 20 minutes in clean, fresh water, 1 teaspoon baking soda, and 1 teaspoon black pepper. Drain and cook the bird as you normally would.

ROAST WILD DUCK OR GOOSE

Pluck and dress the birds according to "How to Dress Birds", cut off tail, removing oil sack. Draw and wipe with damp cloth. Rub inside and outside with salt and pepper. Fill the inside with your favorite poultry stuffing, wild rice stuffing, or you may omit the stuffing and use a small apple, stalk of celery, or a whole onion. You may want to add a little wine and butter to the inside of the bird if you use fruit or vegetables for stuffing. Close the opening using a large carpet needle and strong string such as butchers twine, or you may use small skewers. Truss the wings to the body. Cover the breast with strips of salt pork fat or bacon. Bake breast side up, uncovered in a 300° oven until done. Allow 20 to 25 minutes baking time for each pound. Duck should be served rare; therefore take care not to overcook. Baste frequently with the pan drippings. Serve with gravy made from the pan drippings and giblet stock.

ROAST 'POSSUM

1 (6 to 8-lb.) young 'possum (live weight)	2 lbs. raw sweet potatoes 2 lb. fresh ripe persimmons

(continued)

27408F-99

The flavor of the animal is improved if the animal is caught alive and fed for a week or longer on persimmons, apples, corn berries, etc. Some possum fanciers insist that mashed persimmons and warm water is the best diet (for the possum that is). The 'possum is then killed and dressed in much the same way as a suckling pig. The 'possum is at its best when it is fat; however as much fat as possible should be removed. The head and tail may be left on or removed. Rub the cleaned cavity with onion or sage. Sprinkle with salt and pepper and fill with apple or onion stuffing. In many parts of the Carolinas, a herb seasoned mixture of persimmons, sweet potatoes and bread crumbs, moistened with beef stock, is a favorite stuffing. Truss and place on rack in a shallow pan underside down. Add 2 tablespoons of water and roast in a 300° to 325° oven for 2 to 2½ hours, or till completely well done, basting occasionally with the drippings from the pan. During the last 15 minutes of baking time, place cut up, parboiled sweet potatoes around the 'possum and also baste these with the drippings. Skim the fat from the gravy and serve with stewed persimmons and sweet potatoes. Will feed 6 to 8.

ROAD KILL STEW

I started not to put this dish (if you care to call it that) in my book, but after thinking about it, I decided to, because someone on down the line surely will. Back during the depression years of the 1930's, a lot of people had very little food to eat and fresh, safe meat was almost non-existent to them. They resorted to picking up fresh killed animals, such as rabbit, squirrel, raccoons and opossums, from the side of the road, I regret to say that in some areas of this country, it is still being done. Some states have passed laws against this practice, to discourage it. Under no circumstance should animals be picked up from roads or highways to be eaten, they could be diseased or poisoned. Leave the disposal to the highway department; their people are trained to handle this job properly.

CHICKEN FEET WITH LIVERS AND GIZZARDS

4 to 6 chicken feet	½ tsp. black pepper
10 chicken livers	2 T. chicken fat
10 chicken gizzards	3 c. water
½ tsp. salt	2 T. all-purpose flour

(continued)

27408F-99

Bring water to a boil in a cast iron frying pan. Drop chicken feet in boiling water and cook for 5 minutes. Remove the skin and toenails and return to frying pan. Add livers, gizzards, salt, pepper and chicken fat. Blend flour with ¼ cup of water and set aside. Bring mixture in frying pan back to a boil, reduce heat to a simmer, cover with a lid and cook for 20 minutes. Gradually add flour and water mixture to the frying pan, stirring constantly until thickened. Serve over biscuits with fried apples on the side. Serves 2 to 4.

STEWED SQUIRREL WITH GRAVY

2 squirrels, skinned, cleaned and
   quartered
1½ tsp. salt
2 c. + ½ c. water

1 c. evaporated milk
3 T. all-purpose flour
¼ tsp. black pepper

Place cut up squirrels in a 2-quart pot with 2 cups water, salt and pepper. Cover and simmer until tender, about 1 hour. Remove squirrels from the pot and add evaporated milk to the broth. Mix ½ cup water with the flour and blend until smooth. Gradually add flour mixture to milk and broth mixture stirring constantly. Continue stirring until broth thickens. Add squirrels back to the pot, cover and continue to cook over low heat, stirring about every 10 minutes. Serve over hot biscuits. Have plenty of biscuits on the side for sopping. Serves 4 the first time you make it, only 2 the second time.

BAKED RABBIT

2 to 3 pound dressed rabbit, cut
   into serving pieces*
¼ c. flour
2 tsp. salt
⅛ tsp. pepper

¼ c. melted lard
⅓ c. sliced onions
2 c. chicken or rabbit stock
2 T. water

Combine ¼ cup of flour with salt and pepper. Roll rabbit pieces into seasoned flour. Heat the lard in a Dutch oven and cook onions until tender. Remove the onions from the Dutch oven and brown the rabbit pieces in the same fat. Spread the cooked onions over the rabbit pieces in the Dutch oven. Add the stock to the Dutch oven. Cover the Dutch oven with a lid and bake in a 350° oven for 1½ hours. Remove rabbit pieces to a serving platter and keep warm. Strain liquid from the Dutch oven, removing solids. Return liquid to the Dutch oven. In a small bowl

(continued)

combine ¼ cup water and 2 tablespoons flour and stir until all lumps disappear, add this mixture to the liquid in the Dutch oven, stirring while mixing. Bring mixture in the Dutch oven to a slow boil stirring continuously until thickened to make gravy. Pour the gravy over the rabbit pieces. Makes about 6 servings. *Wild or domestic rabbit may be used, wild rabbit has a gamey taste, if this is offensive to you, soak the rabbit pieces in cold salt water for about 4 hours.

RECIPE FAVORITES

INDEX OF RECIPES

Breads & Rolls

Pies, Pastry & Desserts

Cakes, Cookies & Candy

This & That

How to Order

Get your additional copies of this cookbook by returning an order form and your check or money order to:

Jerry G. Smith
P.O. Box 262
Harbinger, NC 27941
(252) 491-2403

Please send me _____ copies of the **Cooking Seafood and Carolina Critters** at **$9.95** per copy and **$2.00** for shipping and handling per book. Enclosed is my check or money order for $_____.

Mail Books To:

Name _____

Address _____

City _____ State _____ Zip _____

Please send me _____ prints of the **The Cape Hatteras Lighthouse,** 10 x 12 matted at **$13.00** per print and **$2.50** for shipping and handling per print. Enclosed is my check or money order for $_____.

Mail Books To:

Name _____

Address _____

City _____ State _____ Zip _____

Cooking Tips

1. After stewing a chicken, cool in broth before cutting into chunks; it will have twice the flavor.

2. To slice meat into thin strips, as for stir-fry dishes, partially freeze it so it will slice more easily.

3. A roast with the bone in will cook faster than a boneless roast. The bone carries the heat to the inside more quickly.

4. When making a roast, place dry onion soup mix in the bottom of your roaster pan. After removing the roast, add 1 can of mushroom soup and you will have a good brown gravy.

5. For a juicier hamburger, add cold water to the beef before grilling (½ cup to 1 pound of meat).

6. To freeze meatballs, place them on a cookie sheet until frozen. Place in plastic bags. They will stay separated so that you may remove as many as you want.

7. To keep cauliflower white while cooking, add a little milk to the water.

8. When boiling corn, add sugar to the water instead of salt. Salt will toughen the corn.

9. To ripen tomatoes, put them in a brown paper bag in a dark pantry, and they will ripen.

10. To keep celery crisp, stand it upright in a pitcher of cold, salted water and refrigerate.

11. When cooking cabbage, place a small tin cup or can half full of vinegar on the stove near the cabbage. It will absorb the odor.

12. Potatoes soaked in salt water for 20 minutes before baking will bake more rapidly.

13. Let raw potatoes stand in cold water for at least a half-hour before frying in order to improve the crispness of French-fried potatoes. Dry potatoes thoroughly before adding to oil.

14. Use greased muffin tins as molds when baking stuffed green peppers.

15. A few drops of lemon juice in the water will whiten boiled potatoes.

16. Buy mushrooms before they "open." When stems and caps are attached firmly, mushrooms are truly fresh.

17. Do not use metal bowls when mixing salads. Use wood, glass or china.

18. Lettuce keeps better if you store it in the refrigerator without washing it. Keep the leaves dry. Wash lettuce the day you are going to use it.

19. Do not use soda to keep vegetables green. It destroys Vitamin C.

20. Do not despair if you oversalt gravy. Stir in some instant mashed potatoes to repair the damage. Just add a little more liquid in order to offset the thickening.

Herbs & Spices

Acquaint yourself with herbs and spices. Add in small amounts, ¼ teaspoon for every 4 servings. Crush dried herbs or snip fresh ones before using. Use 3 times more fresh herbs if substituting fresh for dried.

Basil   Sweet, warm flavor with an aromatic odor. Use whole or ground. Good with lamb, fish, roast, stews, ground beef, vegetables, dressing and omelets.

Bay Leaves   Pungent flavor. Use whole leaf but remove before serving. Good in vegetable dishes, seafood, stews and pickles.

Caraway   Spicy taste and aromatic smell. Use in cakes, breads, soups, cheese and sauerkraut.

Chives   Sweet, mild flavor like that of onion. Excellent in salads, fish, soups and potatoes.

Cilantro   Use fresh. Excellent in salads, fish, chicken, rice, beans and Mexican dishes.

Curry Powder   Spices are combined to proper proportions to give a distinct flavor to meat, poultry, fish and vegetables.

Dill   Both seeds and leaves are flavorful. Leaves may be used as a garnish or cooked with fish, soup, dressings, potatoes and beans. Leaves or the whole plant may be used to flavor pickles.

Fennel   Sweet, hot flavor. Both seeds and leaves are used. Use in small quantities in pies and baked goods. Leaves can be boiled with fish.

Ginger   A pungent root, this aromatic spice is sold fresh, dried or ground. Use in pickles, preserves, cakes, cookies, soups and meat dishes.

Herbs & Spices

Marjoram   May be used both dried or green. Use to flavor fish, poultry, omelets, lamb, stew, stuffing and tomato juice.

Mint   Aromatic with a cool flavor. Excellent in beverages, fish, lamb, cheese, soup, peas, carrots, and fruit desserts.

Oregano   Strong, aromatic odor. Use whole or ground in tomato juice, fish, eggs, pizza, omelets, chili, stew, gravy, poultry and vegetables.

Paprika   A bright red pepper, this spice is used in meat, vegetables and soups or as a garnish for potatoes, salads or eggs.

Parsley   Best when used fresh, but can be used dried as a garnish or as a seasoning. Try in fish, omelets, soup, meat, stuffing and mixed greens.

Rosemary   Very aromatic. Can be used fresh or dried. Season fish, stuffing, beef, lamb, poultry, onions, eggs, bread and potatoes. Great in dressings.

Saffron   Orange-yellow in color, this spice flavors or colors foods. Use in soup, chicken, rice and breads.

Sage   Use fresh or dried. The flowers are sometimes used in salads. May be used in tomato juice, fish, omelets, beef, poultry, stuffing, cheese spreads and breads.

Tarragon   Leaves have a pungent, hot taste. Use to flavor sauces, salads, fish, poultry, tomatoes, eggs, green beans, carrots and dressings.

Thyme   Sprinkle leaves on fish or poultry before broiling or baking. Throw a few sprigs directly on coals shortly before meat is finished grilling.

Baking Breads

Hints for Baking Breads

1. Kneading dough for 30 seconds after mixing improves the texture of baking powder biscuits.

2. Instead of shortening, use cooking or salad oil in waffles and hot cakes.

3. When bread is baking, a small dish of water in the oven will help keep the crust from hardening.

4. Dip a spoon in hot water to measure shortening, butter, etc., and the fat will slip out more easily.

5. Small amounts of leftover corn may be added to pancake batter for variety.

6. To make bread crumbs, use the fine cutter of a food grinder and tie a large paper bag over the spout in order to prevent flying crumbs.

7. When you are doing any sort of baking, you get better results if you remember to preheat your cookie sheet, muffin tins or cake pans.

Rules for Use of Leavening Agents

1. In simple flour mixtures, use 2 teaspoons baking powder to leaven 1 cup flour. Reduce this amount 1/2 teaspoon for each egg used.

2. To 1 teaspoon soda use 2 1/4 teaspoons cream of tartar, 2 cups freshly soured milk, or 1 cup molasses.

3. To substitute soda and an acid for baking powder, divide the amount of baking powder by 4. Take that as your measure and add acid according to rule 2.

Proportions of Baking Powder to Flour

biscuits ....to 1 cup flour use 1 1/4 tsp. baking powder
cake with oil ....to 1 cup flour use 1 tsp. baking powder
muffins ....to 1 cup flour use 1 1/2 tsp. baking powder
popovers ....to 1 cup flour use 1 1/4 tsp. baking powder
waffles ....to 1 cup flour use 1 1/4 tsp. baking powder

Proportions of Liquid to Flour

drop batter ....to 1 cup liquid use 2 to 2 1/2 cups flour
pour batter ....to 1 cup liquid use 1 cup flour
soft dough ....to 1 cup liquid use 3 to 3 1/2 cups flour
stiff dough ....to 1 cup liquid use 4 cups flour

Time and Temperature Chart

Breads	Minutes	Temperature
biscuits	12 - 15	400° - 450°
cornbread	25 - 30	400° - 425°
gingerbread	40 - 50	350° - 370°
loaf	50 - 60	350° - 400°
nut bread	50 - 75	350°
popovers	30 - 40	425° - 450°
rolls	20 - 30	400° - 450°

Baking Desserts

Perfect Cookies

Cookie dough that is to be rolled is much easier to handle after it has been refrigerated for 10 to 30 minutes. This keeps the dough from sticking, even though it may be soft. If not done, the soft dough may require more flour and too much flour makes cookies hard and brittle. Place on a floured board only as much dough as can be easily managed.

Flour the rolling pin slightly and roll lightly to desired thickness. Cut shapes close together and add trimmings to dough that needs to be rolled. Place pans or sheets in upper third of oven. Watch cookies carefully while baking in order to avoid burned edges. When sprinkling sugar on cookies, try putting it into a salt shaker in order to save time.

Perfect Pies

1. Pie crust will be better and easier to make if all the ingredients are cool.

2. The lower crust should be placed in the pan so that it covers the surface smoothly. Air pockets beneath the surface will push the crust out of shape while baking.

3. Folding the top crust over the lower crust before crimping will keep juices in the pie.

4. In making custard pie, bake at a high temperature for about ten minutes to prevent a soggy crust. Then finish baking at a low temperature.

5. When making cream pie, sprinkle crust with powdered sugar in order to prevent it from becoming soggy.

Perfect Cakes

1. Fill cake pans two-thirds full and spread batter into corners and sides, leaving a slight hollow in the center.

2. Cake is done when it shrinks from the sides of the pan or if it springs back when touched lightly with the finger.

3. After removing a cake from the oven, place it on a rack for about five minutes. Then, the sides should be loosened and the cake turned out on a rack in order to finish cooling.

4. Do not frost cakes until thoroughly cool.

5. Icing will remain where you put it if you sprinkle cake with powdered sugar first.

Time and Temperature Chart

Dessert	Time	Temperature
butter cake, layer	20-40 min.	380° - 400°
butter cake, loaf	40-60 min.	360° - 400°
cake, angel	50-60 min.	300° - 360°
cake, fruit	3-4 hrs.	275° - 325°
cake, sponge	40-60 min.	300° - 350°
cookies, molasses	18-20 min.	350° - 375°
cookies, thin	10-12 min.	380° - 390°
cream puffs	45-60 min.	300° - 350°
meringue	40-60 min.	250° - 300°
pie crust	20-40 min.	400° - 500°

Vegetables & Fruits

Vegetable	Cooking Method	Time
artichokes	boiled	40 min.
	steamed	45-60 min.
asparagus tips	boiled	10-15 min.
beans, lima	boiled	20-40 min.
	steamed	60 min.
beans, string	boiled	15-35 min.
	steamed	60 min.
beets, old	boiled or steamed	1-2 hours
beets, young with skin	boiled	30 min.
	steamed	60 min.
	baked	70-90 min.
broccoli, flowerets	boiled	5-10 min.
broccoli, stems	boiled	20-30 min.
brussels sprouts	boiled	20-30 min.
cabbage, chopped	boiled	10-20 min.
	steamed	25 min.
carrots, cut across	boiled	8-10 min.
	steamed	40 min.
cauliflower, flowerets	boiled	8-10 min.
cauliflower, stem down	boiled	20-30 min.
corn, green, tender	boiled	5-10 min.
	steamed	15 min.
	baked	20 min.
corn on the cob	boiled	8-10 min.
	steamed	15 min.
eggplant, whole	boiled	30 min.
	steamed	40 min.
	baked	45 min.
parsnips	boiled	25-40 min.
	steamed	60 min.
	baked	60-75 min.
peas, green	boiled or steamed	5-15 min.
potatoes	boiled	20-40 min.
	steamed	60 min.
	baked	45-60 min.
pumpkin or squash	boiled	20-40 min.
	steamed	45 min.
	baked	60 min.
tomatoes	boiled	5-15 min.
turnips	boiled	25-40 min.

Drying Time Table

Fruit	Sugar or Honey	Cooking Time
apricots	1/4 c. for each cup of fruit	about 40 min.
figs	1 T. for each cup of fruit	about 30 min.
peaches	1/4 c. for each cup of fruit	about 45 min.
prunes	2 T. for each cup of fruit	about 45 min.

Vegetables & Fruits

Buying Fresh Vegetables

Artichokes: Look for compact, tightly closed heads with green, clean-looking leaves. Avoid those with leaves that are brown or separated.

Asparagus: Stalks should be tender and firm; tips should be close and compact. Choose the stalks with very little white; they are more tender. Use asparagus soon because it toughens rapidly.

Beans, Snap: Those with small seeds inside the pods are best. Avoid beans with dry-looking pods.

Broccoli, Brussels Sprouts and Cauliflower: Flower clusters on broccoli and cauliflower should be tight and close together. Brussels sprouts should be firm and compact. Smudgy, dirty spots may indicate pests or disease.

Cabbage and Head Lettuce: Choose heads that are heavy for their size. Avoid cabbage with worm holes and lettuce with discoloration or soft rot.

Cucumbers: Choose long, slender cucumbers for best quality. May be dark or medium green, but yellow ones are undesirable.

Mushrooms: Caps should be closed around the stems. Avoid black or brown gills.

Peas and Lima Beans: Select pods that are well-filled but not bulging. Avoid dried, spotted, yellow, or flabby pods.

Buying Fresh Fruits

Bananas: Skin should be free of bruises and black or brown spots. Purchase them green and allow them to ripen at home at room temperature.

Berries: Select plump, solid berries with good color. Avoid stained containers which indicate wet or leaky berries. Berries with clinging caps, such as blackberries and raspberries, may be unripe. Strawberries without caps may be overripe.

Melons: In cantaloupes, thick, close netting on the rind indicates best quality. Cantaloupes are ripe when the stem scar is smooth and the space between the netting is yellow or yellow-green. They are best when fully ripe with fruity odor.

Honeydews are ripe when rind has creamy to yellowish color and velvety texture. Immature honeydews are whitish-green.

Ripe watermelons have some yellow color on one side. If melons are white or pale green on one side, they are not ripe.

Oranges, Grapefruit and Lemons: Choose those heavy for their size. Smoother, thinner skins usually indicate more juice. Most skin markings do not affect quality. Oranges with a slight greenish tinge may be just as ripe as fully colored ones. Light or greenish-yellow lemons are more tart than deep yellow ones. Avoid citrus fruits showing withered, sunken or soft areas.

Napkin Folding

General Tips:
Use well-starched linen napkins if possible. For more complicated folds, 24-inch napkins work best. Practice the folds with newspapers. Children can help. Once they learn the folds, they will have fun!

Shield

Easy fold. Elegant with monogram in corner.

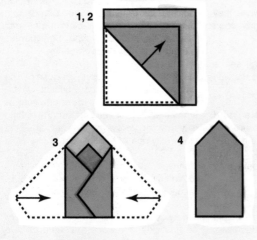

Instructions:
1. Fold into quarter size. If monogrammed, ornate corner should face down.
2. Turn up folded corner three-quarters.
3. Overlap right side and left side points.
4. Turn over; adjust sides so that they are even, single point in center.
5. Place point up or down on plate, or left of plate.

Rosette

Elegant on plate.

Instructions:
1. Fold left and right edges to center, leaving 1/2" opening along center.
2. Pleat firmly from top edge to bottom edge. Sharpen edges with hot iron.
3. Pinch center together. If necessary, use small piece of pipe cleaner to secure and top with single flower.
4. Spread out rosette.

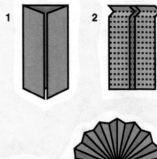

Napkin Folding

Candle

Easy to do; can be decorated.

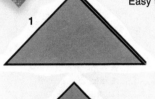

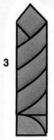

Instructions:
1. Fold into triangle, point at top.
2. Turn lower edge up 1".
3. Turn over, folded edge down.
4. Roll tightly from left to right.
5. Tuck in corner. Stand upright.

Fan

Pretty in napkin ring or on plate.

Instructions:
1. Fold top and bottom edges to center.
2. Fold top and bottom edges to center a second time.
3. Pleat firmly from the left edge. Sharpen edges with hot iron.
4. Spread out fan. Balance flat folds of each side on table. Well-starched napkins will hold shape.

Lily

Effective and pretty on table.

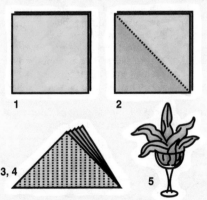

Instructions:
1. Fold napkin into quarters.
2. Fold into triangle, closed corner to open points.
3. Turn two points over to other side. (Two points are on either side of closed point.)
4. Pleat.
5. Place closed end in glass. Pull down two points on each side and shape.

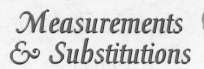

Measurements & Substitutions

Measurements

a pinch	⅛ teaspoon or less
3 teaspoons	1 tablespoon
4 tablespoons	¼ cup
8 tablespoons	½ cup
12 tablespoons	¾ cup
16 tablespoons	1 cup
2 cups	1 pint
4 cups	1 quart
4 quarts	1 gallon
8 quarts	1 peck
4 pecks	1 bushel
16 ounces	1 pound
32 ounces	1 quart
1 ounce liquid	2 tablespoons
8 ounces liquid	1 cup

**Use standard measuring spoons and cups.
All measurements are level.**

Substitutions

Ingredient	Quantity	Substitute
baking powder	1 teaspoon	¼ tsp. baking soda plus ½ tsp. cream of tartar
catsup or chili sauce	1 cup	1 c. tomato sauce plus ½ c. sugar and 2 T. vinegar (for use in cooking)
chocolate	1 square (1 oz.)	3 or 4 T. cocoa plus 1 T. butter
cornstarch	1 tablespoon	2 T. flour or 2 tsp. quick-cooking tapioca
cracker crumbs	¾ cup	1 c. bread crumbs
dates	1 lb.	1 ½ c. dates, pitted and cut
dry mustard	1 teaspoon	1 T. prepared mustard
flour, self-rising	1 cup	1 c. all-purpose flour, ½ tsp. salt, and 1 tsp. baking powder
herbs, fresh	1 tablespoon	1 tsp. dried herbs
milk, sour	1 cup	1 T. lemon juice or vinegar plus sweet milk to make 1 c. (let stand 5 minutes)
whole	1 cup	½ c. evaporated milk plus ½ c. water
min. marshmallows	10	1 lg. marshmallow
onion, fresh	1 small	1 T. instant minced onion, rehydrated
sugar, brown	½ cup	2 T. molasses in ½ c. granulated sugar
powdered	1 cup	1 c. granulated sugar plus 1 tsp. cornstarch
tomato juice	1 cup	½ c. tomato sauce plus ½ c. water

**When substituting cocoa for chocolate in cakes, the amount of flour must
be reduced. Brown and white sugars usually can be interchanged.**

Equivalency Chart

Food	Quantity	Yield
apple	1 medium	1 cup
banana, mashed	1 medium	1/3 cup
bread	1 1/2 slices	1 cup soft crumbs
bread	1 slice	1/4 cup fine, dry crumbs
butter	1 stick or 1/4 pound	1/2 cup
cheese, American, cubed	1 pound	2 2/3 cups
American, grated	1 pound	5 cups
cream cheese	3-ounce package	6 2/3 tablespoons
chocolate, bitter	1 square	1 ounce
cocoa	1 pound	4 cups
coconut	1 1/2 pound package	2 2/3 cups
coffee, ground	1 pound	5 cups
cornmeal	1 pound	3 cups
cornstarch	1 pound	3 cups
crackers, graham	14 squares	1 cup fine crumbs
saltine	28 crackers	1 cup fine crumbs
egg	4-5 whole	1 cup
whites	8-10	1 cup
yolks	10-12	1 cup
evaporated milk	1 cup	3 cups whipped
flour, cake, sifted	1 pound	4 1/2 cups
rye	1 pound	5 cups
white, sifted	1 pound	4 cups
white, unsifted	1 pound	3 3/4 cups
gelatin, flavored	3 1/4 ounces	1/2 cup
unflavored	1/4 ounce	1 tablespoon
lemon	1 medium	3 tablespoon juice
marshmallows	16	1/4 pound
noodles, cooked	8-ounce package	7 cups
uncooked	4 ounces (1 1/2 cups)	2-3 cups cooked
macaroni, cooked	8-ounce package	6 cups
macaroni, uncooked	4 ounces (1 1/4 cups)	2 1/4 cups cooked
spaghetti, uncooked	7 ounces	4 cups cooked
nuts, chopped	1/4 pound	1 cup
almonds	1 pound	3 1/2 cups
walnuts, broken	1 pound	3 cups
walnuts, unshelled	1 pound	1 1/2 to 1 3/4 cups
onion	1 medium	1/2 cup
orange	3-4 medium	1 cup juice
raisins	1 pound	3 1/2 cups
rice, brown	1 cup	4 cups cooked
converted	1 cup	3 1/2 cups cooked
regular	1 cup	3 cups cooked
wild	1 cup	4 cups cooked
sugar, brown	1 pound	2 1/2 cups
powdered	1 pound	3 1/2 cups
white	1 pound	2 cups
vanilla wafers	22	1 cup fine crumbs
zwieback, crumbled	4	1 cups

Food Quantities
For Large Servings

	25 Servings	50 Servings	100 Servings
Beverages:			
coffee	½ pound and 1 ½ gallons water	1 pound and 3 gallons water	2 pounds and 6 gallons water
lemonade	10-15 lemons and 1 ½ gallons water	20-30 lemons and 3 gallons water	40-60 lemons and 6 gallons water
tea	¹/₁₂ pound and 1 ½ gallons water	¹/₆ pound and 3 gallons water	¹/₃ pound and 6 gallons water
Desserts:			
layered cake	1 12" cake	3 10" cakes	6 10" cakes
sheet cake	1 10" x 12" cake	1 12" x 20" cake	2 12" x 20" cakes
watermelon	37 ½ pounds	75 pounds	150 pounds
whipping cream	¾ pint	1 ½ to 2 pints	3-4 pints
Ice cream:			
brick	3 ¼ quarts	6 ½ quarts	13 quarts
bulk	2 ¼ quarts	4 ½ quarts or 1 ¼ gallons	9 quarts or 2 ½ gallons
Meat, poultry or fish:			
fish	13 pounds	25 pounds	50 pounds
fish, fillets or steak	7 ½ pounds	15 pounds	30 pounds
hamburger	9 pounds	18 pounds	35 pounds
turkey or chicken	13 pounds	25 to 35 pounds	50 to 75 pounds
wieners (beef)	6 ½ pounds	13 pounds	25 pounds
Salads, casseroles:			
baked beans	¾ gallon	1 ¼ gallons	2 ½ gallons
jello salad	¾ gallon	1 ¼ gallons	2 ½ gallons
potato salad	4 ¼ quarts	2 ¼ gallons	4 ½ gallons
scalloped potatoes	4 ½ quarts or 1 12" x 20" pan	9 quarts or 2 ¼ gallons	18 quarts 4 ½ gallons
spaghetti	1 ¼ gallons	2 ½ gallons	5 gallons
Sandwiches:			
bread	50 slices or 3 1-pound loaves	100 slices or 6 1-pound loaves	200 slices or 12 1-pound loaves
butter	½ pound	1 pound	2 pounds
lettuce	1 ½ heads	3 heads	6 heads
mayonnaise	1 cup	2 cups	4 cups
mixed filling			
meat, eggs, fish	1 ½ quarts	3 quarts	6 quarts
jam, jelly	1 quart	2 quarts	4 quarts

Microwave Hints

1. Place an open box of hardened brown sugar in the microwave oven with 1 cup hot water. Microwave on high for 1 1/2 to 2 minutes for 1/2 pound or 2 to 3 minutes for 1 pound.

2. Soften hard ice cream by microwaving at 30% power. One pint will take 15 to 30 seconds; one quart, 30-45 seconds; and one-half gallon, 45-60 seconds.

3. To melt chocolate, place 1/2 pound in glass bowl or measuring cup. Melt uncovered at 50% power for 3-4 minutes; stir after 2 minutes.

4. Soften one 8-ounce package of cream cheese by microwaving at 30% power for 2 to 2 1/2 minutes. One 3-ounce package of cream cheese will soften in 1 1/2 to 2 minutes.

5. A 4 1/2 ounce carton of whipped topping will thaw in 1 minute on the defrost setting. Whipped topping should be slightly firm in the center, but it will blend well when stirred. Do not over thaw!

6. Soften jello that has set up too hard - perhaps you were to chill it until slightly thickened and forgot it. Heat on a low power setting for a very short time.

7. Heat hot packs. A wet fingertip towel will take about 25 seconds. It depends on the temperature of the water used to wet the towel.

8. To scald milk, cook 1 cup for 2 to 2 1/2 minutes, stirring once each minute.

9. To make dry bread crumbs, cut 6 slices of bread into 1/2-inch cubes. Microwave in 3-quart casserole 6-7 minutes, or until dry, stirring after 3 minutes. Crush in blender.

10. Refresh stale potato chips, crackers or other snacks of such type by putting a plateful in the microwave for 30-45 seconds. Let stand for 1 minute to crisp. Cereals can also be crisped.

11. Nuts will be easier to shell if you place 2 cups of nuts in a 1-quart casserole with 1 cup of water. Cook for 4 to 5 minutes and the nutmeats will slip out whole after cracking the shell.

12. Stamp collectors can place a few drops of water on a stamp to remove it from an envelope. Heat in the microwave for 20 seconds, and the stamp will come off.

13. Using a round dish instead of a square one eliminates overcooked corners in baking cakes.

14. Sprinkle a layer of medium, finely chopped walnuts evenly onto the bottom and side of a ring pan or bundt cake pan to enhances the looks and eating quality. Pour in batter and microwave as recipe directs.

15. Do not salt foods on the surface as it causes dehydration and toughens food. Salt after you remove from the oven unless the recipe calls for using salt in the mixture.

16. Heat left-over custard and use it as frosting for a cake.

17. Melt marshmallow creme. Half of a 7-ounce jar will melt in 35-40 seconds on high. Stir to blend.

18. To toast coconut, spread 1/2 cup coconut in a pie plate and cook for 3-4 minutes, stirring every 30 seconds after 2 minutes. Watch closely, as it quickly browns.

19. To melt crystallized honey, heat uncovered jar on high for 30-45 seconds. If jar is large, repeat.

20. One stick of butter or margarine will soften in 1 minute when microwaved at 20% power.

Calorie Counter

Beverages

apple juice, 6 oz. 90
coffee (black) 0
cola type, 12 oz. 115
cranberry juice, 6 oz. 115
ginger ale, 12 oz. 115
grape juice, (prepared from
  frozen concentrate), 6 oz. 142
lemonade, (prepared from
  frozen concentrate), 6 oz. 85
milk, protein fortified, 1 c. 105
  skim, 1 c. 90
  whole, 1 c. 160
orange juice, 6 oz. 85
pineapple juice, unsweetened, 6 oz. 95
root beer, 12 oz. 150
tonic (quinine water) 12 oz. 132

Breads

cornbread, 1 sm. square 130
dumplings, 1 med. 70
French toast, 1 slice 135
melba toast, 1 slice 25
muffins, blueberry, 1 muffin 110
  bran, 1 muffin...............................106
  corn, 1 muffin................................125
  English, 1 muffin 280
pancakes, 1 (4-in.) 60
pumpernickel, 1 slice 75
rye, 1 slice 60
waffle, 1 216
white, 1 slice 60-70
whole wheat, 1 slice 55-65

Cereals

cornflakes, 1 c. 105
cream of wheat, 1 c. 120
oatmeal, 1 c. 148
rice flakes, 1 c. 105
shredded wheat, 1 biscuit 100
sugar krisps, ¾ c. 110

Crackers

graham, 1 cracker 15-30
rye crisp, 1 cracker............................35
saltine, 1 cracker..........................17-20
wheat thins, 1 cracker 9

Dairy Products

butter or margarine, 1 T.....................100
cheese, American, 1 oz. 100
  camembert, 1 oz. 85
  cheddar, 1 oz. 115
  cottage cheese, 1 oz. 30
  mozzarella, 1 oz. 90
  parmesan, 1 oz. 130
  ricotta, 1 oz. 50
  roquefort, 1 oz. 105
  Swiss, 1 oz. 105
cream, light, 1 T. 30
  heavy, 1 T. 55
  sour, 1 T. 45
hot chocolate, with milk, 1 c. 277
milk chocolate, 1 oz. 145-155
yogurt
  made w/ whole milk, 1 c. 150-165
  made w/ skimmed milk, 1 c. 125

Eggs

fried, 1 lg. 100
poached or boiled, 1 lg. 75-80
scrambled or in omelet, 1 lg. 110-130

Fish and Seafood

bass, 4 oz. 105
salmon, broiled or baked, 3 oz. 155
sardines, canned in oil, 3 oz. 170
trout, fried, 3 ½ oz. 220
tuna, in oil, 3 oz. 170
  in water, 3 oz. 110

Calorie Counter

Fruits

apple, 1 med.	80-100
applesauce, sweetened, ½ c.	90-115
unsweetened, ½ c.	50
banana, 1 med.	85
blueberries, ½ c.	45
cantaloupe, ½ c.	24
cherries (pitted), raw, ½ c.	40
grapefruit, ½ med.	55
grapes, ½ c.	35-55
honeydew, ½ c.	55
mango, 1 med.	90
orange, 1 med.	65-75
peach, 1 med.	35
pear, 1 med.	60-100
pineapple, fresh, ½ c.	40
canned in syrup, ½ c.	95
plum, 1 med.	30
strawberries, fresh, ½ c.	30
frozen and sweetened, ½ c.	120-140
tangerine, 1 lg.	39
watermelon, ½ c.	42

Meat and Poultry

beef, ground (lean), 3 oz.	185
roast, 3 oz.	185
chicken, broiled, 3 oz.	115
lamb chop (lean), 3 oz.	175-200
steak, sirloin, 3 oz.	175
tenderloin, 3 oz.	174
top round, 3 oz.	162
turkey, dark meat, 3 oz.	175
white meat, 3 oz.	150
veal, cutlet, 3 oz.	156
roast, 3 oz.	76

Nuts

almonds, 2 T.	105
cashews, 2 T.	100
peanuts, 2 T.	105
peanut butter, 1 T.	95
pecans, 2 T.	95
pistachios, 2 T.	92
walnuts, 2 T.	80

Pasta

macaroni or spaghetti, cooked, ¾ c.	115

Salad Dressings

blue cheese, 1 T.	70
French, 1 T.	65
Italian, 1 T.	80
mayonnaise, 1 T.	100
olive oil, 1 T.	124
Russian, 1 T.	70
salad oil, 1 T.	120

Soups

bean, 1 c.	130-180
beef noodle, 1 c.	70
bouillon and consomme, 1 c.	30
chicken noodle, 1 c.	65
chicken with rice, 1 c.	50
minestrone, 1 c.	80-150
split pea, 1 c.	145-170
tomato with milk, 1 c.	170
vegetable, 1 c.	80-100

Vegetables

asparagus, 1 c.	35
broccoli, cooked, ½ c.	25
cabbage, cooked, ½ c.	15-20
carrots, cooked, ½ c.	25-30
cauliflower, ½ c.	10-15
corn (kernels), ½ c.	70
green beans, 1 c.	30
lettuce, shredded, ½ c.	5
mushrooms, canned, ½ c.	20
onions, cooked, ½ c.	30
peas, cooked, ½ c.	60
potato, baked, 1 med.	90
chips, 8-10	100
mashed, w/milk & butter, 1 c.	200-300
spinach, 1 c.	40
tomato, raw, 1 med.	25
cooked, ½ c.	30

Cooking Terms

Au gratin: Topped with crumbs and/or cheese and browned in oven or under broiler.

Au jus: Served in its own juices.

Baste: To moisten foods during cooking with pan drippings or special sauce in order to add flavor and prevent drying.

Bisque: A thick cream soup.

Blanch: To immerse in rapidly boiling water and allow to cook slightly.

Cream: To soften a fat, especially butter, by beating it at room temperature. Butter and sugar are often creamed together, making a smooth, soft paste.

Crimp: To seal the edges of a two-crust pie either by pinching them at intervals with the fingers or by pressing them together with the tines of a fork.

Crudites: An assortment of raw vegetables (i.e. carrots, broccoli, celery, mushrooms) that is served as an hors d'oeuvre, often accompanied by a dip.

Degrease: To remove fat from the surface of stews, soups, or stock. Usually cooled in the refrigerator so that fat hardens and is easily removed.

Dredge: To coat lightly with flour, cornmeal, etc.

Entree: The main course.

Fold: To incorporate a delicate substance, such as whipped cream or beaten egg whites, into another substance without releasing air bubbles. A spatula is used to gently bring part of the mixture from the bottom of the bowl to the top. The process is repeated, while slowly rotating the bowl, until the ingredients are thoroughly blended.

Glaze: To cover with a glossy coating, such as a melted and somewhat diluted jelly for fruit desserts.

Julienne: To cut vegetables, fruits, or cheeses into match-shaped slivers.

Marinate: To allow food to stand in a liquid in order to tenderize or to add flavor.

Meuniére: Dredged with flour and sautéed in butter.

Mince: To chop food into very small pieces.

Parboil: To boil until partially cooked; to blanch. Usually final cooking in a seasoned sauce follows this procedure.

Pare: To remove the outermost skin of a fruit or vegetable.

Poach: To cook gently in hot liquid kept just below the boiling point.

Purée: To mash foods by hand by rubbing through a sieve or food mill, or by whirling in a blender or food processor until perfectly smooth.

Refresh: To run cold water over food that has been parboiled in order to stop the cooking process quickly.

Sauté: To cook and/or brown food in a small quantity of hot shortening.

Scald: To heat to just below the boiling point, when tiny bubbles appear at the edge of the saucepan.

Simmer: To cook in liquid just below the boiling point. The surface of the liquid should be barely moving, broken from time to time by slowly rising bubbles.

Steep: To let food stand in hot liquid in order to extract or to enhance flavor, like tea in hot water or poached fruit in sugar syrup.

Toss: To combine ingredients with a repeated lifting motion.

Whip: To beat rapidly in order to incorporate air and produce expansion, as in heavy cream or egg whites.